# ROAD ACCI
# COMPENSA

Terence Baldwin took a law degree at Leicester University after a number of years as an engineer in the car industry. He is a solicitor at a large Milton Keynes practice which has a high profile in the field of road accident claims. He would like to see the law being made more understandable and accessible to everyone, and he has contributed to this by teaching introductory law and A level law at evening classes. Terence Baldwin lives in Kettering, Northants and is the author of several books and articles.

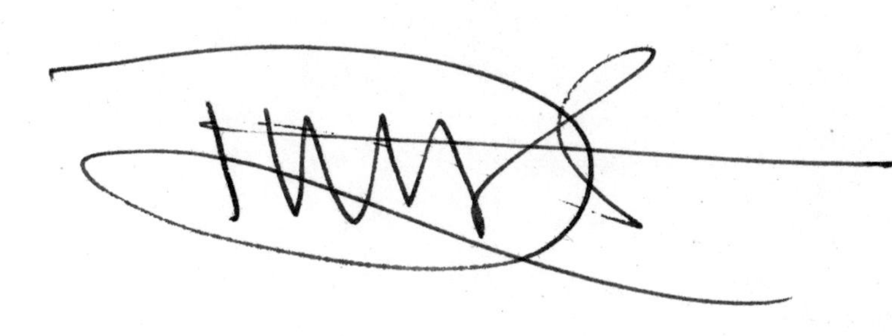

# ROAD ACCIDENT COMPENSATION

TERENCE BALDWIN

ROBERT HALE • LONDON

First published in Great Britain 1996

ISBN 0 7090 5811 X

Robert Hale Limited
Clerkenwell House
Clerkenwell Green
London EC1R 0HT



2 4 6 8 10 9 7 5 3 1

Typeset by Pitfold Design, Hindhead, Surrey.
Printed in Great Britain by St Edmundsbury Press,
Bury St Edmunds, Suffolk.
Bound by WBC Book Manufacturers Ltd,
Bridgend, Mid-Glamorgan.

# CONTENTS

# INTRODUCTION

If you are involved in a road accident which was not your fault, you have a right to be compensated for any resulting injury or other loss. A legal framework exists to help you to obtain compensation, but you will need some assistance to take advantage of it.

According to Department of Transport statistics, there are more than 1,500,000 (yes, one and a half million) road accidents in Britain every year. Of these, some 280,000 involve injury to one or more people. Altogether, about 330,000 people suffer some injury, while many more escape injury but are left with the expense and inconvenience caused by damage to their cars.

It is a regrettable fact that if you travel by road, either as a driver or as a passenger, there is a very real possibility that you will be involved in a road accident at some time. The effect on you, and on your family, can vary from a minor mishap to a major catastrophe.

About 70% of people involved in road accidents are legally entitled to compensation, but it is estimated that only about 30% of these take steps to claim it. The reason for this is likely to be a fear of starting something which they know nothing about and, particularly, what it will cost.

The purpose of this book is to explain how to prepare for the possible need to make a claim for compensation, how your claim is likely to proceed, and the procedures which your solicitor may be involved with. It also explains what he might ask you to do so that progress can be made with your claim. It is not intended to be a guide to DIY litigation, although it may be of considerable help to you if you decide to run your claim yourself without the help of a lawyer. You might do this because you cannot afford to instruct a solicitor, you are not eligible for Legal Aid, you do not have legal costs insurance and you cannot find a solicitor to take your case on a conditional fee basis.

I have tried to provide some answers to the questions you would most like answered: 'What can I claim for? How much will I get? Why does it take so long?'

For simplicity I will refer to all persons as 'he' to avoid the tedious use of 'he or she'. I hope no one will be offended. Where I refer to a driver, this can include the riders of motorcycles and of cycles and horses. The term car is to include any vehicle or mount. The person or persons you would claim against might not have been a driver involved in the accident. It might be a company, a car's owner or even a government department. I refer to the person you would claim against as either the other driver, the defendant or your opponent, depending on the context.

I have tried to avoid being too technical, but I have mentioned some statutes and included details of some cases which illustrate the points they refer to. These may be of help to lawyers who are not familiar with road accident claims, and also to persons running their own claim, as well as being of general interest. You may notice some repetition of certain points concerning what can be claimed and what you should do to prove your claim. These are important points which, I consider, deserve to be repeated at the appropriate places rather than referring you to other chapters too often.

The advice in this book is based on my understanding of the law and rules of court in England and Wales at January 1996. Although there is a different legal system in Scotland, the principles and advice in this book will be just as useful to Scottish readers. Northern Ireland has a legal system which is not very different from that of England. The law and rules are constantly changing, and you should check the current position with a lawyer before taking legal action yourself.

At the time of writing, there are proposals for a fundamental reform of the civil courts and procedures. These, if adopted, may affect time limits, entitlement to costs, and the paperwork. They will not affect the principles and advice in this book for obtaining road accident compensation.


# ACKNOWLEDGEMENTS

I wish to record my thanks to my colleagues in the Fennemores Personal Injury and Private Client departments for their advice and assistance on many points during the preparation of this book. I am particularly grateful to Anne Maguire (for Scottish law and Legal Aid matters), to David Israel (regarding enforcement measures), and to our librarian Alex Reid for his patient help with source material.

I have cited cases from *Current Law* and *Quantum Casewatch* with the permission of the publisher Sweet & Maxwell.

# 1 WHY YOU CAN CLAIM – THE LEGAL BASIS

A claim for compensation for injury, property damage and other financial loss arising from a road accident is most often based on the common law civil wrong of negligence. Common law is that law found in the reports of past cases which is still recognized by the courts, but which is not in a statute passed by Parliament. A civil wrong such as negligence, trespass and battery is called a tort. Battery is also a criminal offence, although it is charged as assault. The criminal law is concerned with wrongs against society in general, whereas the civil law is concerned with claims by individuals against the wrong-doer. The difference between criminal law and civil law is more fully explained in chapter 26.

Other drivers, and also the driver of the car in which you are a passenger, are under a duty to you to drive with the reasonable skill and care of a prudent motorist. The duty includes such things as ensuring that the car is in a safe condition. If the driver fails in this duty and you suffer an injury or financial loss as a direct result, you are entitled to claim compensation, called damages, from that driver. His failure may also be an offence under the Road Traffic Acts, but not necessarily so.

Even if he has caused the accident, the other driver might not be at fault. For example, he might suffer a heart attack which he could not reasonably have foreseen would happen so that he loses control of his car. If you suffer injury or loss as a result, you will not have a claim because the driver was not negligent. The right to compensation depends on someone else being found at fault. So although you will have suffered loss, there would be no one to blame in law. This happened in *Jones* v. *Dennison* (1971). The defendant was driving his car when it mounted the pavement and injured the plaintiff. The driver said that he had suffered a blackout. He had suffered blackouts before, but he did not know it. His wife knew, but she had not told him. The court found that the driver was not to blame for the accident because what had happened to him was outside his control and he could not reasonably have expected it to happen. The innocent plaintiff was not compensated for her injury.

Another example of the other driver not being to blame is where he loses control of his car because of oil on the road. In this case, your claim is likely to be against the person who negligently left the oil, but who is likely to be unknown. It may be possible, in these circumstances, to fix blame on the highway authority if it had been told of the oil spillage but had been slow to clear it up or to place warning signs.

If you are a paying passenger in a taxi or a bus, you have a contract with the operator of the service. Contracts are legally binding agreements, most of them need not be in writing. There is an implied term in the contract that you will pay for the journey, and there is an implied term that the driver will drive carefully. There may be advantages in bringing an action in contract as well as tort, such as claiming for the loss to you caused by not arriving at your destination.

## You have only yourself to blame

You may not be able to claim even if you were not driving. In *Pitts* v. *Hunt* (Court of Appeal 1990) a pillion passenger on a motorcycle encouraged the driver to drive in such a way as to deliberately frighten the public. Both had been drinking. The escapade ended in a crash, and the passenger's claim against his driver failed. They had been engaged in a joint illegal enterprise, and the driver did not owe a duty of care to his passenger in these circumstances.

# 2 WHO TO CLAIM FROM

If the other driver has been negligent and caused you loss, your claim is primarily against him. However, other people may also be liable to compensate you. This will be important if the other driver is not insured and does not have the money to compensate you, or if you cannot find him or, even if you find him, you cannot serve a summons on him for any reason. The person you make your claim against, when legal proceedings are issued, is called the defendant or, in Scotland, the defender.

Care must be taken in choosing the right defendant. In *Worsley* v. *Hollins* (1991) the plaintiff was stationary in traffic when a van ran into the back of him. He sued the van driver and the van's owner. The van driver said that the brakes had failed. It was proved that a vital part was missing which the driver could not have suspected, and he was held not to blame. The van had been fully serviced six weeks before the accident, so the owner had not failed to maintain it properly and he was held not liable. The inference is that someone at the garage which serviced the van had been negligent, but the garage was not a defendant in the action, so the plaintiff's claim failed.

## The defendant has died

Your claim survives the defendant's death and is brought against his estate instead. If he was insured, his insurer will still deal with the claim. If he was not insured, your claim will be a potential debt to be paid out of the assets of his estate. The other driver's personal representatives dealing with his estate should be informed of the claim as soon as possible. If the assets of the estate are not sufficient to satisfy your claim, you will have the same remedy as if the uninsured driver had not died, which is through an application to the Motor Insurers' Bureau (MIB).

If proceedings are issued, a living person must be substituted for the dead defendant. This will usually be a personal representative appointed by his Will, or an application may need to be made to court to have someone appointed as a substitute defendant.

## A bankrupt defendant

A claim arising from a road accident against a defendant who is declared bankrupt is not affected by the bankruptcy as other debts are, and his insurer must pay any judgment made against him. However, you must obtain the leave of the court before issuing proceedings against a bankrupt defendant.

## Learner drivers

A learner driver is required to drive with the same skill and care as any careful and prudent motorist. He cannot escape blame for an accident because of his inexperience. The learner driver's instructor should have some control over the way the car is driven, and you may need to issue proceedings against both the learner driver and his instructor.

## An employer as defendant

If the other driver was driving in the course of his employment, his employer is also responsible for paying your compensation. This is called vicarious liability. The employer is liable for the faults of his employee provided that the negligent act is done in the course of his employment. A delivery driver in his employer's van on a weekday is likely to be driving in the course of his employment, although this should be checked with his employer. The same driver in his van on a Sunday afternoon may be driving for his own purposes rather than those of his employer.

Proceedings are usually taken against both the employer and the driver in case of a problem arising with either one of them. The driver might leave his job and be untraceable so that a summons cannot be served on him. A company is a legal person. It has many of the legal rights and obligations which a natural person has. It can own property, and it can sue and be sued in the name of the company, acting through its directors. It is born when it is incorporated and it dies when it is dissolved. If a company is in liquidation, also called winding-up, it is still alive but its assets are frozen while the liquidator sorts out how they are to be distributed among its creditors. If the other driver's employer is a company which goes into liquidation, the court's approval is needed to take proceedings against the liquidator as he takes the place of the company. Your solicitor will check with the register of companies to see if the company is still trading, before issuing proceedings against it. The company's insurer will deal with the claim once the liquidator is properly served with the summons. A dissolved company can be restored to the register of companies, in effect resurrected, by an order of the court. It can then be sued and its insurer at the time of the accident will be obliged to pay a judgment obtained against the company. A partnership, called a firm, is not a legal person but is a group of natural persons, any one of whom can be sued for the negligent acts of the firm and its employees.

## Foreign motorists

If the other driver is a foreigner, he should have an international certificate of insurance, sometimes called a 'green card'. The issuer of this insurance will appoint an insurance company or a claims handling body in England to deal with the claim. If there is a problem with the foreign motorist's insurance, your claim will be dealt with under the MIB procedure.

## Diplomats

Foreign diplomats have immunity from the jurisdiction of the English courts, provided by the Diplomatic Privileges Act 1964. In other words, you cannot sue them. This immunity extends to their families, and also to the staff of the diplomatic mission when they are going about their duties. So the driver of a diplomatic car has immunity while driving in the course of his duties, but not if he is on his day off. In practice, most diplomatic missions waive this immunity in respect of road accidents and take out insurance. If there is no insurance, and the head of the diplomatic mission does not waive the immunity, you can sue the appropriate government as the other driver's employer. Foreign governments are immune from legal action under the State Immunity Act 1978, but some matters are excluded from the immunity. Liability for death, injury and damage to tangible property is excluded.

## The Crown

If the other driver is employed by a government department, his employer is the Crown. By the Crown Proceedings Act 1947 the Crown is no longer immune from suit, and the Secretary of State of the relevant department should be a defendant if the driver was acting in the course of his employment. If you are in collision with an army lorry, the defendant will be the Ministry of Defence.

## A passenger's own driver

If you were a passenger, your claim may be against the

driver of the car you were in. Even though you might not think that your driver was in any way to blame for the accident, a court may reach a different decision. Your driver might be your spouse, your parent or your adult child. He should be insured and so will not have to compensate you from his own resources. You are an innocent party, and you are entitled to be compensated for your losses by the insurer of either or both of the drivers involved.

You should not feel embarrassed, and your driver ought not to feel victimized, by you making a claim against him. We all make mistakes when driving, and only very few of them result in an accident. You will need to instruct a different firm of solicitors to the one which is dealing with your driver's claim against the other driver because of the possibility of a conflict of interests between you. The same firm of solicitors cannot act in the best interests of both of you if they are pursuing the claim for you while defending that claim for your driver.

## The other car's owner

A car owner has a statutory duty under the Road Traffic Act 1988 to satisfy himself that anyone who drives it is insured. If the owner allows someone to drive his car without checking that the driver is insured, and you suffer loss as a result of the uninsured driver's negligence, you can claim against the car's owner for his breach of statutory duty. You must still prove that the driver was at fault, but the owner would also be liable to pay your damages.

## The passenger defendant

A car passenger might carelessly open his door and damage your car as you pass. He might open it into the path of a cyclist or a pedestrian, causing injury. If there is insurance cover for the car he was in, the insurer will meet your claim because of its obligations under the Road Traffic Act. If there is no insurance, and the passenger does not have personal liability insurance, which is often included in household insurance, you will have to consider whether he is a person worth suing. The MIB will not help you unless the passenger had some measure of control of the car.

## Other defendants

It is not only other drivers who create hazards which cause road accidents. Allowing smoke to obscure visibility on a road is negligent. It is also an offence, under the Highways Act 1980, to light a fire within fifty feet of a road and so would be a breach of statutory duty as well. Farmers' insurers are familiar with claims arising from road accidents involving collisions with escaped animals, or which occur when drivers swerve trying to avoid hitting them.

In *Misell* v. *Essex County Council* (High Court 1994) the plaintiff was a motorcyclist. He suffered injury when he lost control of his machine on a muddy road. The County Council was held liable to him for breach of a statutory duty under the Highways Act 1980 for not taking appropriate steps to minimize the hazard.

# 3 PROVING BLAME FOR THE ACCIDENT

A driver is responsible for his negligent acts. However, it is for the person making a claim against him to establish that he was negligent and wholly (or at least partly) responsible for the accident, and that this negligence caused or contributed to the injury or other loss suffered. An insured driver has a duty to his insurer not to admit liability.

A road accident occurs suddenly and unexpectedly. You will be shaken and confused if you are not actually knocked unconscious or seriously injured, and the future burden of proving liability will not be uppermost in your mind. However, no matter how clear it is to you that the other driver was to blame, it may be quite difficult to prove it. He is likely to tell a completely different story to his own insurer.

## Contributory negligence

Although the other driver may have done a silly thing, such as pulled out of a side road into your path, you might be held to have contributed to the accident by driving fast or not keeping a proper look-out. Even though you have the right of way, you are still obliged to drive with proper care and to try to avoid colliding with the other vehicle. Other examples of possible contributory negligence are:

1 Driving a car which is not roadworthy such as having defective brakes.

2 Not showing lights when it is appropriate to do so, such as when other cars are showing lights. This is

because an unlit vehicle is difficult to see when others are showing lights, since drivers may pick out the lit cars but miss the unlit ones. The official lighting-up times are not relevant to this issue; while it is not a criminal offence not to show lights in the daytime, it may be negligent.

3 Driving too fast. The speed limit for the road might not be relevant. While speeding is a criminal offence, it is not negligent if it did not contribute to the accident. However, driving within the speed limit, but too fast for the particular circumstances, is likely to be held negligent when an accident occurs. This might be when driving in heavy traffic or negotiating a tight bend.

4 Using a mobile telephone while driving.

5 Giving a misleading signal. This happens if your signal does not cancel after a turn or you signal to turn but then change your mind. A driver waiting to emerge from a side road should not rely on a signalled intention to turn made by a driver on the main road, but both drivers are likely to be found to have contributed to a a resulting accident.

In *Wadsworth* v. *Gillespie* (1978) the defendant, waiting at a junction, saw a motorcycle approaching from her right. The motorcycle's left indicator was operating. The defendant pulled out into the main road, relying on the motorcyclist's signalled intention to turn left, but he drove straight on and a collision occurred. The Highway Code advises that you do not assume that a vehicle will turn left although it is signalling that intention. The motorcyclist was held one-third to blame.

In *Powell* v. *Moody* (CA 1966) the plaintiff was riding his motorcycle along the outside of two lines of stationary traffic. A car was let out of a side road on the left by the traffic ahead of the plaintiff, and he collided with it. The judge held the plaintiff 80% to blame for the accident, and this was upheld on appeal. It is common practice for motorcyclists to overtake stationary traffic, taking advantage of their narrow width. The courts consider this to be 'jumping the queue' and fraught with hazard.

The other driver's insurer may offer to deal with your claim on a split liability basis. This is expressed in terms of percentages such as 50:50 or 75:25. If you accept this, the value of your claim would be reduced by the same percentage as the apportionment of liability you accepted. Your insurer would be obliged to deal with any claim from the other driver on the same terms. You should not agree an apportionment of liability without your insurer's agreement.

## The facts speak for themselves

The burden of proving his claim is usually on the plaintiff, and the defendant can remain passive, he need not prove anything unless he is counter-claiming. The exception to this is where the facts themselves point to the defendant being negligent. Lawyers refer to this as the doctrine of *res ipsa loquitur* – the thing speaks for itself. In such a case, the court is entitled to infer the defendant's negligence from the facts unless he can show that there is some other explanation.

In *Chapman* v. *Copeland* (1966) the plaintiff's husband was riding his moped across a twenty-four foot wide carriageway. He had travelled seventeen of the twenty-four feet when he was hit and killed by a car driven by the defendant. His car had left skid marks 184 feet long on the road. The defendant declined to give evidence of what happened, and relied on there being no oral evidence against him. The judge decided that the skid marks were evidence which 'spoke' against the defendant, who had not suggested in court that the moped rider had done anything wrong which could be an alternative explanation for the accident.

## Witnesses

The most compelling evidence to support your version of events is the testimony of one or more independent witnesses. These are persons who were not in any of the vehicles involved in the accident, and who are not connected in any way with any of the people who were involved. If possible, you should ask such persons at the scene of the accident if they saw it happen, what they saw and who they thought was to blame. Ask them if they would assist you by being a witness, and write down their name and address. Do this even if the police are at the scene. Often the police do not record details at an accident scene if there is no obvious injury to anyone.

All drivers are obliged by law to give their name and address and, if someone else is injured, details of their insurer, to any person having reasonable cause to require them, unless they report the accident to the police. It is a criminal offence, under section 170 of the Road Traffic Act 1988, to refuse to do so.

About 10% of all drivers are uninsured, and many of them give a false name and address at the accident scene. Ask to see some proof of identity and, if you are not satisfied, contact the police immediately. It is advisable to report the accident to the police in any case, and strongly request that details of the accident be recorded. Unfortunately, the police are not obliged to comply with your request. They will often take no interest in the accident if it does not involve injury to anyone.

It is a good idea to carry a camera loaded with film in your car. It need not be an expensive one. A photograph of the accident scene, of any skid marks and of the damage to the respective cars, can be invaluable when liability is disputed, and for identifying the other driver if it becomes necessary to trace him. The camera should have a flash and batteries, in case of an accident at night. If you do not have a camera with you, at least make a sketch of the road with the positions of the cars and any skid marks, and showing where the damage is on the cars. Ask the other driver to agree the sketch and sign it. If he refuses, or is not able to talk to you, ask a witness to sign it as being correct. Your solicitor will arrange for professional agents to visit the accident site and compile a photographic and sketch plan report, called a locus in quo report, if liability is disputed. It will have details such as the road width which will supplement your photographs or sketch. The road layout may change soon after the accident so that an accurate professional locus report is not possible. Sometimes a report will be compiled by the police accident investigation department. There can be a considerable delay before a police report becomes available. They are not released until any criminal proceedings are completed.

The other driver may allege that the accident was your fault, or at least partly your fault. He may start legal proceedings against you first, or enter a counter-claim when you issue proceedings against him. If he begins legal proceedings first, you may receive a summons and other papers. Pass these to your insurance company immediately. Unless a defence is entered within fourteen days, the other driver may obtain a judgment against you.

Beware of the driver who offers to pay for the repairs to your car himself. In most cases this is a ploy to get you to delay reporting the accident to your own insurer and getting professional help with your claim. The 'private payer' will rapidly lose his keenness to settle your claim once he has left the accident scene.

I recognize that my advice about what to do immediately following an accident requires you to be thinking clearly, when in fact you are likely be shocked and dazed. However, I hope that some of these points will occur to you at the accident scene and so save you considerable trouble later. Taking appropriate steps at the time may possibly even save your claim from failing because the other driver has disappeared, or because you have no evidence to support your claim against him.

If the other driver is convicted of a driving offence, the conviction is supportive evidence of his negligence, but it is not conclusive. If he is acquitted of the charge, that is not evidence that he was *not* negligent. It means that there is insufficient evidence for a criminal conviction, which requires a higher standard of proof than does a civil claim.

# 4 PROVING BLAME FOR YOUR LOSSES

## Proving causation

You must not only prove that the other driver has caused the accident because of his negligence. You must also prove that his negligence caused your injury and other losses. The link between the accident and your losses is called the chain of causation. It must lead from the negligence to the loss claimed. It is tested by asking the question, 'But for the accident, would I have suffered this loss?' If the accident is not the sole cause of the loss, you cannot claim that loss as a consequence of the accident.

***Example 1***
You suffer an injury in the accident, and you claim for, among other things, a loss of overtime earnings. You had the benefit of this overtime before the accident. Your employer is asked about overtime, and he says that the demand for the company's products has declined and overtime has been stopped. To the test question, 'But for the accident, would I have lost overtime earnings?', the answer is 'yes'. The accident has not caused the loss of overtime.

***Example 2***
You booked a cruise to the Caribbean before the accident. Because of your injuries, you cannot go on the cruise and you claim for loss of enjoyment of it. You then receive a letter from the travel agent saying that the cruise is cancelled because of, for instance, war in the Caribbean. The loss of the holiday is not caused by the accident because it was cancelled anyway.

You may be involved in a second incident which is a direct consequence of the first. An example is where your leg is injured in a road accident. Despite being careful, your injured leg gives way and you fall heavily, breaking your arm. Because the second accident was a direct consequence of the first accident, there is no break in the chain of causation. You can add your broken arm to your claim in respect of the road accident. In *Wieland* v. *Cyril Lord Carpets Ltd* (High Court 1969) a woman suffered a neck injury in a road accident. She wore a support collar which made her hold her head in such a way that it was difficult to keep her spectacles on. Because of this, she could not judge distances which led to her falling down some steps and suffering further injury. The court held that the fall was a foreseeable consequence of the injury sustained in the road accident.

## The intervening act

If the chain of causation is broken by a new event, the other driver cannot be blamed for the losses caused by the new event. This is called variously a supervening act, a superseding act, or by its latin tag *novus actus interveniens* – a new intervening act. You may be unfortunate enough to be involved in a second accident. This might break the chain of causation between the first accident and the losses you claim. The pain and suffering arising from the first accident may be superseded by equal or worse injuries caused by the second accident. Perhaps you could not work and lost earnings because of the first accident, and you also could not work because of injuries sustained in the second accident. In both cases, your claim against the driver involved in the first accident is likely to end at the date of the second accident, which is a new intervening act.

The intervening act could be a disease which overtakes you, rendering you as incapacitated as the accident left you. It could be leaving your damaged car in the open for a long period such that it deteriorates. The loss of value of the car caused by the accident is overtaken by the deterioration caused by your own neglect. Damage by vandals might also be an intervening act. The effect of an intervening act can be to reduce the further liability of the person who caused your original injury or losses from the date of the second incident, or to eliminate it altogether.

It is very important that you tell your solicitor about any further injury, disease or change of circumstances which arises after the accident which gave rise to your claim. He can then advise you about its relevance to your claim.

## Remoteness of damage

Although your injury or other loss is a direct consequence of the accident, you will not be compensated for it if it is of a type that one would not reasonably expect could be caused by the accident. The defendant is only liable for losses which were reasonably foreseeable before the accident. In *Meah* v. *McCreamer* (High Court 1985) the plaintiff had suffered a head injury in a road accident. This caused a personality change to the extent that he committed crimes. Two of his victims successfully sued him for damages arising from his crimes. He sought to recover the sum he paid out in damages from the driver who caused his personality change. This claim was held to be too remote from the defendant's negligent driving.

The courts can sometimes be generous and allow claims for rather remote losses. In *Jones* v. *Jones* (1984) the facts were not too far removed from those of *Meah* v. *McCreamer.* Mr Jones sustained a head injury in a road accident causing a personality change. Because of this, his wife sought a divorce. He was able to add the cost of the divorce settlement to his claim. The court decided that this possibility was foreseeable.

# 5 WHERE THE MONEY COMES FROM

## I – INSURERS

It is a legal requirement that all drivers have third-party insurance cover. A third party is anyone who is not a party to the insurance contract between you (and any other drivers covered by your policy) and the insurance company. The insurer and the insured are first and second parties.

Third parties who can claim against you include not only drivers and passengers involved in the accident, and car owners who were not in their car at the time, but also the owners of other property which has been damaged. The local authority can claim for damage to traffic bollards and road signs, and British Telecom can claim for damage to telegraph poles. Building owners can claim for damage to their garden walls.

If you have comprehensive insurance, your insurer will settle the repair costs of your car. If it is uneconomical to repair, – a 'write-off' – you will receive its agreed pre-accident value. This is not the sum you paid for the car, nor is it the same as what a replacement car will cost you. The pre-accident value is determined by motor vehicle assessors as being what they think the car was worth having regard to its condition and appeal on the open market. Your insurer may instead make an offer of settlement for your car based on the trade value, what a dealer would pay, found in *Glass's Guide*. This is a motor trade publication not available to the public. You can find an indication of car values in the specialist magazines, such as *Parker's Guide* which are stocked by many newsagents. It will be close enough to *Glass's* for practical purposes. It might be possible to persuade your insurance company to increase its offer by obtaining your own professional valuation. If you still cannot agree on the value, you will have to take legal action against your insurer for breach of contract in not paying you an adequate sum for your car's value. This would not be advisable except in very clear cases where there is convincing evidence that your insurer is undervaluing your car. The Insurance Ombudsman might be able to suggest an acceptable compromise. The role of the Ombudsman is discussed later in this chapter.

Your comprehensive policy may also cover you for charges for recovering your car from the scene of the accident and taking it to a garage or place of storage, and also the storage charges until the car has been inspected. Some policies cover the policyholder's personal belongings against loss or damage up to a maximum total value, often £100. This may overlap with your household insurance. It is worth checking to see that you are not paying twice for the same cover as you cannot claim from both insurers for the same loss. You will have to bear any policy excess, it will be deducted from the payment which your insurer makes. You should add the policy excess sum to your claim.

Your insurer will attempt to recover its outlay to you from the other driver's insurer if he was at fault. It will be claimed in your name under a right known as subrogation. A 'knock-for-knock' agreement means that the two insurers have each agreed to deal with the claim of their own insured driver, rather than looking to the other insurer for recovery of their outlay, as this saves on administration costs. You will lose your no claims bonus. This is a reward for making no claims, it is not a no *fault* bonus. However, if the insurer recovers its outlay or, where there is a knock-for-knock agreement and you are completely successful in your claim against the other driver, your no claims bonus will usually be reinstated. It is a discretionary bonus, and the insurer is under no obligation to restore it.

Your insurance will cover third party claims. Your insurer will also reimburse you for any emergency treatment fee which you must pay for medical treatment for yourself and any passengers following a road accident. This provision is in section 158 of the Road Traffic Act 1988. Your policy may also cover you for fire damage and theft of your car. This type of cover costs more than a bare third party policy but much less than a comprehensive one. A third party, fire and theft policy is often indicated by the initial letters TPFT. All other losses such as injury, loss of earnings and damaged personal property except property covered in a comprehensive policy are uninsured losses, and you must pursue a claim against the other driver, although in practice you are likely to be dealing with his insurer. If liability is not disputed, the other driver drops out of the picture.

The other driver's insurer may be his employer. Large corporations which have the resources to meet any likely claims can be self-insurers. Known self-insurers include the Post Office, British Telecom, the Metropolitan Police and some local authorities.

## The RTA insurer

If the other driver is not insured, but there is valid insurance for the car he was driving although not covering him, the insurer is required to pay such judgment sum as you are awarded against the other driver, under the provisions of the Road Traffic Act. Written notice must be given to the insurer of an intention to issue proceedings, not later than seven days after issue, if they are to be liable to pay the judgment. In practice, the insurer will try to reach a negotiated settlement with you if you have a reasonable prospect of obtaining a judgment. The RTA insurer is not required to deal with the claim of an injured passenger who has allowed himself to be carried in a stolen car.

## The domestic agreement insurer

The insurer might be able to avoid indemnifying the other driver because of some irregularity, such as not disclosing past motoring convictions. The agreement provides for an insurer who would have indemnified the driver but for the irregularity to pay a judgment obtained against that driver by a third party. The insurer can then look to the uninsured motorist to reimburse its outlay. This differs from the Motor Insurers' Bureau scheme discussed in chapter 6, which takes effect when there is no insurer connected with the other driver.

## Your own indemnity

You are required to provide your own insurer with all relevant information to enable them to assess the risk they will undertake in covering you against claims by third parties. This is a continuing obligation which does not only apply at the time of arranging the insurance.

If you do not advise your insurer of relevant facts such as a driving conviction or poor health, the insurance company can declare the insurance invalid at any time including after you have been involved in an accident. The insurer can refuse to cover you against a claim. In such a case, your insurance company will settle any justifiable claim brought against you, but it may then seek reimbursement from you for its outlay.

You must ensure that you comply with the conditions in your insurance policy if the cover is to be effective. This is largely a matter of common sense. In *Clarke* v. *National Insurance and Guarantee Corpn Ltd* (High Court 1963), a driver carried eight passengers in his four-seater car. A term of his insurance policy excluded the use of the car in an unsafe condition. The driver's insurer refused to meet claims arising from an accident involving the heavily overloaded car under the policy, so that he lost his claim to be indemnified.

You must report any accident you are involved in to your insurer, even if you are not going to claim on your insurance. This is a material fact which your insurer needs to know in order to assess the risk of insuring you, and the appropriate premium to charge.

## The insurance ombudsman

The Insurance Ombudsman Bureau was set up by the insurance industry to provide a simple and inexpensive means of resolving disputes between member companies of the Bureau and their policyholders. The independence of the Ombudsman is ensured by a council made up of representatives of consumers and other interests as well as of member companies.

If you have a dispute with your insurance company, which might be about indemnity cover, or an inadequate offer in respect of insured losses, you should first take it up with the senior management of the company. If the dispute is not resolved, you can write with full details to the insurance Ombudsman. You must do this within six months of receiving the final decision in the matter from your insurance company. The Ombudsman, or his deputy, will investigate your complaint and try to resolve the dispute by agreement. If this is not possible, he will state his view of how the dispute should be resolved. You are not bound to accept his decision.

You cannot ask the Ombudsman to intervene in disputes about the cost of insurance, or about your dissatisfaction with the other driver's insurer, or if you have already issued legal proceedings about the dispute. The Ombudsman's services are free.

## Insurance brokers

Your only contact with your insurer may be through an insurance broker. Brokers know the motor insurance market and will recommend an appropriate policy to you. Brokers bring together the parties to the insurance contract, being you and your insurer. They are not the agents of either party. If the insurance proposal form is filled out for you by the broker, it is essential that you check that all details are correct before you sign it. If anything is wrong, your insurer can refuse to indemnify you.

Insurance brokers can offer a range of additional protection which is not provided by your car insurance policy, and the cost is usually quite modest. These include legal costs insurance, which is discussed in chapter 14, and credit car hire. A credit car hire arrangement will provide you with a hire car after an accident at no cost to you while your own is being repaired, or for up to about three weeks while you look for a replacement car. The credit hire company will hope to get the hire charges from the other driver. The arrangement will only take effect if the other driver is likely to be held to blame for the accident, if he is insured, and his insurance details are known. You will claim for the hire charges, and pass the money you receive to the credit hire company. If you comply with the terms of the credit hire agreement but you do not recover all or some of the hire charges, the credit hire company will take the loss.

Insurance brokers can be very helpful when you have an accident. They can advise you on the initial steps and may assist you in pushing matters along. However, they are not insurers, or claims handlers, or qualified to give legal advice.

# 6 WHERE THE MONEY COMES FROM

## II – UNINSURED DRIVERS AND THE MIB

It is estimated that about 10% of motorists are not insured. The seeming reluctance of the Crown Prosecution Service and the police to prosecute, and the very low fines generally imposed by Magistrates, can make it an economic proposition to drive uninsured for persons who have no assets with which to pay a claim. Proposals have been put to Parliament to introduce the compulsory display of an insurance disc in the car windscreen as evidence that the car is covered by insurance. This is a positive move towards reducing the number of uninsured drivers.

If the other driver is uninsured, your claim will be dealt with by an insurer nominated by the Motor Insurers' Bureau (MIB). This organization obtains its funds from the insurance companies which, in turn, add about £50 to the premiums which the dutiful majority of motorists have to pay. It is a fund of last resort which will compensate innocent victims of road accidents if the person who is liable to compensate them does not have the means to pay the judgment sum, or cannot be traced. You will not be eligible to benefit from the MIB scheme if you were yourself an uninsured driver involved in the accident, or you were a passenger and you knew that your driver was not insured. He will not be insured if he has taken the car without the consent of its owner.

You should complete an MIB application form as soon as you know or suspect that the other driver was not insured. If the other driver cannot even be traced, you can still submit a claim to the MIB, but you will get nothing for property damage. In the case of an uninsured (but traced) driver, you will not recover the first £175 of your claim for property damage. This is a form of 'policy excess' applied by the MIB to filter out very low value claims. The MIB will also deal with your claim if the other driver's insurance company goes out of business. It will not pay subrogated claims. These are sums paid to you by, for instance, your employer as sick pay or a health insurer such as BUPA. These may require you to add their outlay to your claim and to repay the money if you are successful in recovering it. Since you will not get this money from the MIB, you will not be required to repay it. You can get the appropriate application form, for uninsured driver or untraced driver, from the Motor Insurers' Bureau, whose address can be found at p. 154.

The MIB will want to attempt to recover the money which it has paid to you from the uninsured motorist. It will require you to transfer to it your right of legal action against the uninsured driver and anyone else who might be liable to compensate you. These possible defendants are discussed in chapter 2. Your right of action is transferred by signing a form of assignment supplied by MIB, which then decides whether to pursue the uninsured driver or some other person by court action to recover the money paid to you. You may be required to give a statement and, possibly, to attend court to give evidence of the circumstances of the accident and of your injury or other losses. If the MIB considers it worthwhile pursuing the uninsured motorist to a court hearing, it will have stepped into your shoes in respect of your legal rights, but it will need your assistance as a witness.

The MIB is only required to pay such judgment as you obtain against an uninsured driver. You do not claim against the MIB, although it can choose to be added as a defendant to your action. It might do this so that it can raise defences or allege contributory negligence against you. It would also mean that the MIB can claim reimbursement of the money it pays to you from the uninsured driver without having to start a fresh action. There will usually be an attempt to reach a negotiated settlement with a view to saving the cost of a trial.

In the case of an untraced driver, you do not have a named person whom you can take legal action against. The MIB will assess your claim and make an award. If you reject this award, you can appeal. Your appeal will be considered by an arbitrator, who will be a Queen's Counsel selected by the Secretary of State for the Environment. Before any award is made, you must prove the nature of the injuries and and that they were caused by the accident, and also prove your injury-related losses such as loss of earnings, just as in any other case. The MIB does not pay interest in connection with awards. It does not pay certain costs such as for a police report, and only a nominal sum will be paid towards your solicitor's fee. You must therefore expect your award to be reduced by some of the costs of making the claim.

## The private payer

There are rare cases where the defendant is not insured and the MIB will not be involved. This might be where the defendant is a cyclist or the owner of an animal which has caused the accident. You will need to satisfy yourself that the defendant appears to have the means to pay your claim before you begin. This can involve searching the registers of bankruptcies and county court judgments. You can also search at the land registry, which will reveal the names of the owners of an address and also details of any financial charges against the property, such as a mortgage. There are specialist agents who can do this for you for a reasonable fee.

# 7 WHAT YOU CAN CLAIM FOR

## I – VEHICLE AND OTHER PROPERTY DAMAGE

You are entitled to recover losses directly arising from the accident, provided that the nature of the losses are ones which might reasonably be expected to be suffered as a result of the accident. You must prove by some means that it is more likely than not that you suffered the losses claimed, and that they were caused by the accident. This is a lower standard of proof than is required in criminal matters where facts must be proven beyond reasonable doubt.

You can claim for the following heads of damage known as 'General Damages' which are losses implied by the circumstances of the accident, and where no specific value can be established by means of documentary evidence such as receipts or quotations:

1 *Inconvenience.* You will be put to a lot of trouble by the need to arrange car repairs or storage, obtain quotes and valuations and to instruct solicitors in respect of your claim. The other driver's insurer, or the trial judge, should be asked to make a nominal award in respect of this.

2 *Loss of use of your car.* While your car is awaiting repair and being repaired or, if your car is a 'write-off', for the time until you could replace it, you are deprived of the benefit of being able to use your car. This includes the benefit of being able to lend it to someone else. You cannot claim for loss of use for any period while you hired a car.

3 *Diminution in value.* If your car has been repaired, it is likely to be worth less than it was before the repair

simply because a repaired car is less attractive to a potential buyer than is a car which has never been damaged. This will usually only apply to cars up to four years old.

You can also claim for reimbursement of losses and expenses which are not implied, and the value of which can usually be established. These are known as Special Damages:

***Examples***

1. Recovery of your car from the accident scene.
2. Storage of your car pending inspection by the insurers.
3. Insurance policy excess.
4. Car repairs.
5. Pre-accident value of your car if it is uneconomical to repair.
6. Car hire.
7. Taxi, rail and bus fares.
8. Damaged clothing or other possessions.
9. Cost of a holiday. Where a holiday was booked but you were unable to take it due to the accident, you can claim any lost deposit, or the full cost paid and forfeited, and any incidental expenses.
10. Postage and telephone expenses.

Item 10 is really part of your litigation costs which are discussed in chapter 15, but this item is often claimed and paid as special damages. The cost of your time is a litigation cost and never claimed as special damages. If you have instructed a solicitor, only the cost of his time can be claimed as costs. Chapter 15 explains costs in detail.

You cannot claim for interest charges on money you have had to borrow while waiting for your claim to settle. However, you can claim interest on your award of damages at trial. The current rates of interest usually allowed by the courts are 8% on special damages from the date of the loss, and 2% on general damages from the date of issue of proceedings.

A company or firm cannot sue for loss of profit due to injury to its employee. In *IRC* v. *Hambrook* in the Court of Appeal, Lord Denning said 'the loss to A arising out of an injury whereby B is unable to perform his contract (with A) is not actionable.'

## Contractual losses

If you are travelling in a taxi which is involved in an accident and which is the taxi driver's fault, your claim can be based on the contract of carriage you have with him. You have a legal agreement with him, a contract, with the implied terms that he will drive carefully and get you to your destination within a reasonable time. Other terms may be incorporated into the contract. You might tell the driver that you have to catch the 9.30 train to London for your job or you will lose earnings. If he causes an accident so that you miss the train and cannot get another one, you can claim for your lost earnings. The driver must be aware of the prospective loss you face if he lets you down.

## Mitigation of loss

You are not entitled to sit back and let your losses mount. You must take all reasonable steps to mitigate your losses, that is, to keep them to a minimum.

You must try to get your car repaired as soon as possible. Do not wait for the other driver or his insurer to admit liability or to pay you compensation before getting your car repaired and out of storage. Allow your opponent a reasonable time to arrange an inspection of your car, twenty-one days should be sufficient. Obtain at least two estimates of the cost of repair and accept the cheapest. Give your opponent the opportunity of agreeing the repair cost with you to avoid a dispute about it later.

If your car is a 'write-off', you must replace it as soon as you reasonably can. The wreck must be disposed of for the best available salvage price quickly to limit storage charges. The tax disc should be surrendered for a refund of the value of the unexpired months. Insurers will rarely give a refund of the insurance premium for the unexpired time on the policy. This is because they are at risk of a claim as soon as the insurance cover commences. When you start driving again, the insurance cover can be transferred to the replacement car. If you cannot drive again for many months, it may be worth asking for a proportion of the insurance premium in negotiations, but the grounds for claiming it are weak.

You should contact your own insurer as soon as possible after the accident and complete an accident report form. Your own insurer will only deal with insured losses such as your potential liability to a third party, your emergency medical fees and, if you have comprehensive insurance, the repairs or pre-accident value of your car. Some policies cover additional losses such as windscreen replacement and limited property damage. Few motorists are fully aware of the nature and extent of their insurance cover. You are not obliged to claim on your insurance cover, and you can instead add the insured losses to your claim, but you are likely to have to wait very much longer for the money. Also, you cannot claim interest on the value of these items if you fail to mitigate the loss by claiming on your insurance.

# 8 WHAT YOU CAN CLAIM FOR

## I – PERSONAL INJURY AND ASSOCIATED LOSSES

Much of what has been said about the principles relating to claims for property damage in chapter 7 is repeated here in respect of personal injury. This is because persons such as passengers who have no property damage claim are likely to skip that chapter and turn instead directly to this one.

You are entitled to recover losses directly arising from the accident, provided that the nature of the losses are ones which might reasonably be expected to be suffered as a result of the accident. You must prove by some means that it is more likely than not that you suffered the losses claimed, and that they were caused by the accident.

You can claim for the following heads of damage known as 'General Damages' where no specific value can be established by means of documentary evidence such as receipts or wage slips:

1. Physical injury such as cuts, bruising, broken bones, strains causing stiffness or aching, neurological problems due to damage to nerves.

2. Psychological injury, which is a clinically definable injury such as post-traumatic stress disorder. You cannot recover damages for a simple shaking up, fear or anxiety unless you also have suffered a physical injury. This was confirmed by the Court of Appeal in *Nichols* v. *Rushton* in 1992.

3. Loss of amenity, which means that your injury has prevented you from pursuing your normal activities such as general mobility, housework,

sports, hobbies and your pre-accident opportunity to enjoy life generally.

4 Loss of congenial employment, which means that your injury has caused you to change your job to one which is less suitable or satisfying.

5 Disability on the labour market, which means that you are likely to be less attractive as a potential employee, because of your injury, than would be another person with the same qualifications and experience but without the injury.

6 Loss of promotion prospects, where you are more likely to be passed over for promotion in your job than would have been the case before you suffered the injury.

7 Loss of employment protection rights. If you have to find another job, you will not have protection from unfair dismissal, or any right to compensation for redundancy, for the first two years.

8 Loss of holiday enjoyment, where you had already planned a holiday before the accident and you went ahead with it afterwards, but your injury spoiled your enjoyment of the holiday. Alternatively, your disappointment at having to miss the holiday because of your injury.

9 General inconvenience in having to make a claim to compensate you for your losses.

You can also claim for reimbursement of losses and expenses, the value of which can usually be established. These are known as Special Damages:

1 Past loss of earnings.

2 Lost unemployment benefit. This can be treated as a loss of earnings.

3 Contractual sick pay, where you are obliged by contract to reimburse your employer out of your compensation for sick pay received.

4 Statutory sick pay, where an element of your pay which has continued to be paid by your employer has been SSP, and this is going to be deducted from your compensation under the CRU rules discussed in chapter 19.

5 Future loss of earnings, where you are still not back at work or where you are obliged to take a job at lower pay.

6 Loss of pension entitlement due to your change of job or early retirement.

7 Loss of the benefit of a company car. This is found from published tables and is subject to a deduction for tax. You cannot claim for loss of the benefit of an expense account because that is paid to you to offset costs arising from your work and, if you are not working, those costs will not arise.

8 Past and future cost of medicines and medical treatment, including any sums claimed on behalf of a medical expenses insurer.

9 Past and future cost of nursing care.

10 Cost of help with housework, gardening, decorating.

11 Cost of travel to attend for medical treatment.

12 Cost of travel to medical examinations.

13 Postage and telephone expenses.

Items 12 and 13 are really part of the litigation costs to be claimed together with other disbursements and fees at the conclusion of the claim, but they are often included and paid as special damages. Except in exceptional cases, it is not necessary to itemize the cost of telephone calls and letters sent. A nominal sum of £10–£20 is usual, depending on the length of time the case takes to settle or go to trial. The cost of your time is a litigation cost, never an item of damages. If you have instructed a solicitor to progress your claim, you cannot claim your time as well as his. Chapter 15 explains costs in detail. Note that hospital emergency treatment fees will be refunded by your own insurer.

You cannot claim for interest charges on money you have had to borrow while waiting for your claim to settle. However, you can claim interest on your award of damages in respect of past losses but not on future losses such as earnings and medical treatment. The current rates of interest usually allowed by the courts are 8% on special damages from the date of the loss, and 2% on general damages from the date of issue of proceedings.

## Mitigation of loss

You are not entitled to sit back and let your losses mount. You must take all reasonable steps to mitigate your losses, that is, to keep them to a minimum.

If you lose your job because of your injury, you must try to get another suitable job as soon as possible. Keep copies of your letters of application and the replies, and any other evidence of your attempts to find work. If you are successful in getting another job but the pay is less or the expense of doing it such as travel to work is more, you can claim for this financial loss for a reasonable time into the future. You should have appropriate medical treatment.

# 9 PROVING YOUR CLAIM

It is for the person making a claim to show that all of the losses he claims were caused by the accident. The other driver's insurer is unlikely to pay for a claimed loss if they think you would not be able to persuade a judge at trial that the item claimed is a loss arising from the accident, and that the sum claimed is reasonable. Your solicitor can write to various people for documentary evidence in support of your claim, but you can do it just as well if not better, and almost certainly earlier, than he can.

The need for documentary evidence is well illustrated by the observation of Lord Goddard in the case of *Bonham-Carter* v. *Hyde Park Hotel Ltd* (High Court 1948):

> Plaintiffs must understand that, if they wish to bring actions for damages, it is for them to prove their damage; it is not enough to write down particulars and, so to speak, throw them at the court, saying 'This is what I have lost; I ask you to give me these damages.' They have to prove it.

## 1 The car

You will need the receipt for the cost of repairs, and also two other estimates to show that you took steps to have your car repaired as cheaply as was reasonable. If the car is a 'write-off', its pre-accident value and its present value as scrap must be established by a vehicle assessor's report. Your own insurer, or the other driver's insurer, may arrange for this, or you can do it yourself.

It is misleading to look at the prices of similar cars offered for sale, since many factors affect a car's value, and the valuation is on an objective basis and takes no account of what it was worth to you in terms of sentimental value. You will not recover any sums recently spent on the car as maintenance such as a new clutch or tyres. These are expenses necessary to keep the car roadworthy and are included in the pre-accident (roadworthy) valuation.

## 2 Bus and rail travel

Collect all tickets for public transport journeys caused by your accident, such as visits to the doctor or hospital. If you cannot use your car because of its damage or because you cannot drive it, then it would be reasonable to use public transport for your journeys instead and to claim the cost. Taxi journeys must be justifiable. I recommend that you keep a diary after your accident so that you can compile a schedule of journeys from it.

Staple the tickets and receipts to plain sheets of paper, eight or ten to a sheet if space allows, and write a brief note of the purpose of the journey next to the ticket or receipt. Your solicitor can then photocopy the sheets for sending to the other side.

## 3 Personal property

The items of clothing and other personal possessions damaged in the accident should be kept for inspection. Original receipts are to be preferred, but few people keep these. You may be required to show some evidence of having owned the item claimed.

The insurance companies are accustomed to dealing with many fraudulent claims and they expect to see reasonable evidence such as receipts, or photographs which include the item claimed. Receipts for the cost of replacing the items may be acceptable, together with a statement from a person who is independent, that is, not a relative or friend, that you owned the item in question before the accident. This kind of evidence is not required in every case and, for inexpensive items, your word may be acceptable if the item claimed is one likely to have been with you at the time of the accident; for example, while a child's pushchair is not unusual car luggage, a computer is.

Many people claim for items which they say were stolen from their car after the accident. It is difficult to prove that this loss is a direct consequence of the accident that could not reasonably have been prevented by taking appropriate security precautions.

## 4 Loss of earnings

You must establish that you have lost earnings by means of a pre-accident earnings history. Payslips for the previous thirteen weeks are required as a minimum. Some insurers want to see records for twenty-six weeks. In more serious cases, it might be necessary for you to provide P60s (the certificate of pay, tax and National Insurance contributions you receive at the end of each tax year) and full details of your education, training and previous employment, to establish your past income and your future prospects. If you cannot continue to do the work you were doing before the accident, an employment consultant's report might be advisable. This would consider the types of work appropriate for you, the pay rates and the availability of such work in your area.

A child can have a claim for loss of future earnings or of career prospects. Evidence should he presented of his potential by way of school reports, his parents' or other family members' careers, any ambitions he had and by statistics such as average earnings.

## 5 Medical evidence

Your claim for compensation for your injury, and for the losses caused by it such as loss of earnings, must be supported by reports from the appropriate medical specialists. Examples of medical specialists are:

*Chiropractor* – for subtle biomechanical disturbance of the spine.
*Neurologist* – for problems connected with the nervous system such as headaches and blackouts.
*Ophthalmologist* – for eye problems, often associated with head injuries.
*Orthopaedic surgeon* – for bone and soft tissue injuries, fractures, joint pain, whiplash injury.
*Psychiatrist* – for mental disorders such as post-traumatic stress and depression.
*Psychologist* – for functional disorders such as poor memory and recognition skills.

It is not uncommon for injured persons to disagree with a report prepared by a medical expert who has examined them. This may be because the report is objective and reflects the clinical findings at the examination, and recites any history of relevant problems which are noted in their medical records. It is common, and natural, to attribute all pain and discomfort experienced after an accident to that accident. However, neckache, backache and headache are experienced by most of the population, who do not have a recent accident to blame. Also, the mind can play tricks. The pain is real enough, but there is no organic cause.

However, if you think that the report is seriously wrong, your solicitor can ask the medical expert to consider your comments and to amend the report if he thinks it appropriate. He will not amend it simply to satisfy you, as his report is his independent expert opinion. If you are still not satisfied with the report, you will have to write off the cost of it and commission a fresh report from another medical expert.

# 10 FATAL ACCIDENTS AND POSTHUMOUS CLAIMS

This chapter considers claims where a person dies as a result of an accident, or dies from some other cause but having a right to make a claim concerning the accident.

## The deceased's claim

A right to compensation does not die with the claimant. It passes to his personal representative, someone who takes over the legal rights of the person who has died, for the benefit of his estate. This applies whether death was caused by the accident or some other cause.

You cannot claim for the fact of death itself, better described as a loss of expectation of life. The deceased's personal representative can claim on behalf of the estate for the same losses as the deceased would have claimed had he not died, but with any claim for pain, suffering and loss of amenity, and for loss of earnings, limited to the pre-death period. The cost of the funeral, if paid out of the estate, can also be claimed. You should not, therefore, volunteer to pay the cost of the funeral, but instead you can lend the money to the estate. It can then be recovered as a claimable expense of the estate under the Fatal Accidents Act. The legal costs of administering the estate are not normally recoverable. The exception is where sometimes the deceased's assets are of little value so that no formal administration of the estate would have been necessary. The fact that a claim is being made means that it is essential that someone be appointed to legally represent the estate and pursue the claim on its behalf. In this case, the cost of administration directly arises from the litigation and can be recovered, but as costs rather than damages.

## The relatives' claim

You cannot claim for the loss of someone, except for a statutory bereavement award in the case of a spouse or child. This is fixed at £7,500. It is not claimable in respect of an adult child. Where a child under the age of eighteen is married, the award is payable to his spouse. An unmarried partner of at least two years is regarded as a spouse for the purpose of a bereavement award.

## The dependants' claim

People who were financially dependent on the person who has died can claim for their financial loss caused by the death. This is usually a spouse and infant children, but can be financially dependent parents. Claims can be made by adult children who can show dependency. This might only be for gardening, decorating or baby-sitting services given free by the deceased before the accident. The claim will be for the cost of replacing those services. A claim for loss of dependency is likely to fail if the deceased's income was derived from crime.

## Your own claim

If you are a plaintiff bringing claims on behalf of a deceased's estate and dependents, and you have also suffered injury or other loss arising from the accident, you can include this in the same action. You will need to obtain the court's leave to be the plaintiff in two different capacities, in your personal capacity and also as a personal representative, but the granting of leave is usually only a formality.

# 11 ACCIDENTS ABROAD

If you are involved in an accident abroad, your ability to obtain compensation from the other driver's insurer is likely to depend on you being able to get a court judgment against that driver. Taking legal action against a driver in a foreign court which applies laws which may be very different from English laws, can make pursuing a claim somewhat more difficult than usual. You will need to instruct lawyers in the country in which you bring your action. Your own solicitor will assist you with this.

## Where to sue

If the other driver is a citizen of a member state of the European Community, you can sue him in his own country or in the country where the accident occurred, if different. As an example, if you are involved in an accident with a Danish driver in France, you can sue either in Denmark or France, although in both cases French law applies. This European Community provision is incorporated into United Kingdom law by the Civil Jurisdiction and Judgments Act 1982.

In the case of an accident between two English drivers anywhere in the world, if both drivers are normally resident in England, the action could be brought in England on the basis that it is more convenient to the parties. It is also likely that English law would be applied. In *Boys* v. *Chaplin* (House of Lords 1970) there was a road accident in Malta involving two British servicemen who were stationed there. The action was brought after they had returned to England. Both parties agreed to the trial being in

England, but it would have been an advantage to the defendant to apply Maltese law because the damages allowed would have been less. The Law Lords agreed that English law was appropriate in the case, but they each gave a different reason for reaching that conclusion. The general conclusion is that the case had everything to do with England and nothing to do with Malta apart from the coincidence of where the accident occurred.

In the USA, each state has its own laws. If you are involved in an accident in California with a driver from Arizona, you may want to consider both states' laws to see which is the most advantageous to you before starting your action in that state. Some US states do not allow a passenger to sue his own driver. An injured passenger might have to look at the laws of the state where the accident occurred, and of the driver's home state, to see which will allow him to claim against the negligent driver.

# 12 CLAIMS BY CHILDREN AND THE MENTALLY DISABLED

All persons under the age of eighteen are known to the law as minors or infants. They, and other persons certified by a doctor as being incapable of managing their affairs, cannot bring a legal action in their own name. They are 'persons under a disability'. A person who is under a disability sues in the name of another person who is competent at law. This means that he is of full age and mental capacity. He is known as the 'next friend' or, in Scotland, the 'curator bonis'. For a child, this is usually a parent, but it need not be. There must be no conflict of interest between the minor and his next friend. For instance, a defendant to the minor's action could be a parent, in which case neither parent can be his next friend.

The limitation period, the time from the accident to when proceedings must be issued, does not begin to run until the disability is removed. For a child, the disability is removed on his eighteenth birthday. For a person under a mental disability, which means that he is incapable of managing his affairs due to old age, unconsciousness or some other cause, it is when a doctor certifies his recovery. For simplicity, I will now refer only to children, but the matters discussed will apply also to adult persons under a mental disability.

A next friend must deliver to the court a form consenting to act for the child, and also agreeing to pay any costs awarded against the child. The agreement to pay costs is to protect a defendant who succeeds in his defence and is awarded the costs of defending the action, since a child is unlikely to be able to pay those costs. In the case of an adult under a mental disability, since he is unable to consent to the action being taken on his behalf, he will not have consented to the risk of costs. If a child is being sued, he defends the action by a person called his 'guardian ad litem', which means his guardian for the purpose of the litigation. Here is an example of the wording of a form of consent and an undertaking in respect of costs.

***Example***

IN THE NEWTOWN COUNTY COURT CASE NO. N00771

BETWEEN

John Green Plaintiff
(A Minor suing by his Father
and Next Friend DAVID GREEN)

And

Peter Black Defendant

**CONSENT AND UNDERTAKING OF NEXT FRIEND**

I David Green of 12 Nelson Avenue, Potters Bar, Hertfordshire, being the Father of John Green who is a minor and the above named Plaintiff who wishes to commence an action in this Court against Peter Black, consent to be the next friend to John Green and I HEREBY UNDERTAKE to be responsible for the costs of this action as follows, namely that if John Green fails to pay to the proposed Defendant Peter Black when and in such manner as this Court shall order, all such costs of this action as the Court directs him to pay to the said Peter Black, I will forthwith pay the same into the office of this Court.

Dated this . . . day of . . . . . . . . . . . . . . . . . . . . . . . . . 19 . . .

Signed: . . . . . . . . . . . . . . . . . . . . . . . . . . . . . . . . . . . . . . . .

SIGNED BY THE ABOVE NAMED IN MY PRESENCE

. . . . . . . . . . . . . . . . . . . . . . . . . . . . . . . . . . . . . . . . . . . . . .

Solicitor / An officer of the court

An out-of-court settlement for a child must be approved by the court. A special hearing will be arranged for this purpose. The judge will consider the medical evidence and a barrister's opinion on what the proper level of award of money ought to be. He will either approve the proposed settlement, or he will give directions for the continuation of the claim. If the judge approves the proposed settlement, he will require the money to be paid into court. It will be invested on behalf of the child until he reaches eighteen. If the child has a need for the money for his education or welfare before reaching eighteen, his next friend can apply to court for some or all of the money to be paid out.

If the infant settlement is small, less than £500, the costs of an infant settlement hearing are not really justified. In such a case, a parental indemnity may be enough. The child's parent agrees to pay the child's claim if he makes one after he reaches age eighteen, which protects the defendant and his insurer from a fresh claim from the child when he reaches adulthood. Here is an appropriate example of a parent's discharge:

> I, David Green of 12 Nelson Avenue, Potters Bar, Hertfordshire acknowledge that I have received from Peter Black per Rightdrive Insurance Company the sum of £300 (three hundred pounds) in full and final settlement of all claims for personal injuries, loss, damage and expenses both before and after today arising out of an accident in which my son John Green was involved on 11th May 1994 AND it is admitted that this payment is made with a denial of liability. In consideration of the above mentioned payment I, the said David Green, hereby irrevocably undertake to keep the said Peter Black free and indemnified from and against all claims which may be made by or on behalf of my son John arising out of this accident.
>
> Signed:....................
>
> Date:.....................

Some insurance companies want the discharge to be signed by a witness, although it is not a document which needs to be signed in front of a witness to be legally binding. The inclusion of an admission that the defendant denies liability despite settling the claim is a usual requirement of insurance companies. It has no real practical relevance other than to prevent John from obtaining a judgment on liability on the basis of the payment when he reaches the age of eighteen.

Any money received on behalf of a child in settlement of his claim should be deposited in a bank or building society or some other very low risk investment. You may not spend the money, or gamble with it on risky investments. You are a trustee, and the laws on trusteeship are very strict. The Trustee Investments Act 1961 sets out the types of investment which are authorized. Some forms of investment may not be made without first obtaining professional advice. Permitted investments include government securities and some classes of company shares. It is a complex subject and you are strongly advised to obtain professional advice before investing any trust money and also on your duties as a trustee. On reaching his majority, the child can demand that you account to him for the settlement money and reasonable interest.

## The Court of Protection

If a person under a mental disability has a substantial claim, it will be necessary to involve the Court of Protection. This is an office of the Supreme Court which is run by the Public Trust Office. Its function is to exercise control of the financial affairs of mentally disabled persons, called patients by the court.

The court will appoint a person, called a receiver, to be responsible for managing the patient's affairs. The receiver is often the patient's relative or friend, but can be some other appropriate person such as a solicitor, although a person acting in his professional capacity will expect to be paid for the work involved. The receiver must report to the court any substantial sums received for the benefit of the patient, and the court will give directions. The receiver is usually required to prepare accounts of the patient's affairs and send them to the court every year and on the patient's death. The court will charge fees, and the receiver is entitled to claim reasonable expenses, both being payable by the patient.

On a minor reaching eighteen, and on an adult recovering from a mental disability, they can take over any proceedings which have been issued. A notice of adoption of proceedings is filed at court.

# 13 LAWYERS – WHAT THEY ARE AND HOW AND WHEN TO INSTRUCT THEM

Your claim is based on a legal right and is pursued by means of a procedure set out in the rules of court. But proving a claim takes much more than legal knowledge. It requires an ability to assess the medical evidence, to investigate and calculate other losses, and to negotiate a realistic settlement with insurers and their solicitors. There is also the need to be able to present the case in court to its best advantage if the case goes to a hearing.

'Lawyer' is a general term applied to any person who is qualified in the law, and includes solicitors, barristers, judges, legal executives and academic lawyers teaching in colleges and universities. The lawyers who take instructions from the public, obtain evidence and prepare the case for settlement or trial are solicitors. They can also present your case in the county court, but must qualify by examination and experience to have a right of audience in the higher courts such as the High Court and the Court of Appeal.

## Solicitors

The title of solicitor was adopted when attorneys, solicitors and proctors, who each practised in the different courts of the time, were amalgamated in 1873. They are officers of the court, their full title being solicitor of the Supreme Court. Most solicitors are graduates, although there are other routes for entry to the profession. After gaining a degree, usually in law, they then study legal practice for their solicitors' examinations followed by two years of training under articles with a solicitor, a form of apprenticeship. Some solicitors have a degree in another discipline and then study law before the legal practice course. On completion of his training, the trainee is admitted to the Roll of Solicitors, nominally kept by the Master of the Rolls, the chief judge of the civil appeals court. For serious breaches of the rules governing solicitors, their name can be struck off the Roll.

Solicitors usually practise either alone or in partnership with other solicitors. This type of practice is known as a firm, not a company. However, solicitors are now allowed to form companies, which are separate legal entities from the solicitors themselves, and this may become a more common arrangement.

You should instruct a firm of solicitors which is experienced in handling road accident claims. If you have legal costs insurance, that insurer will probably nominate a firm of solicitors which is a member of its panel of approved firms. The Law Society has set up a help line to put you in touch with an appropriate solicitor in your area. The scheme is called the Accident Line, and the freephone telephone number is listed under Useful Addresses (at p. 154).

Your claim may be dealt with by a person who is not a solicitor. He may be a legal executive who has studied law and legal practice and been admitted to membership of the Institute of Legal Executives. They are taking the place of people who used to be known as solicitors' senior clerks. He may be a trainee solicitor or another category of claims handler. These persons will be supervised by a solicitor, and my references to 'solicitor' will include these other categories of staff in the solicitors' office.

You may find your case being passed to another person to deal with on several occasions. This can be unwelcome, but it is probably unavoidable. Apart from staff members leaving and joining a solicitor's firm during the time it takes to build your case, it may need a different specialist to take it over as particular complexities develop.

An indication of quality of experience in dealing with

personal injury claims is where at least one solicitor at the firm is a member of the Law Society's panel of personal injury specialists. He will have satisfied the Law Society, the solicitor profession's supervising body, that he has at least three years of experience of regularly dealing with personal injury work and that he has a satisfactory quality monitoring system in place.

Arrange to instruct a solicitor as soon as possible. Much of the evidence which you need to prove your claim may be lost to you if you delay. For example, injuries such as cuts and bruises should be professionally photographed before they fade, a photographic report of the accident site may be required before road alterations make it difficult to record it accurately, and the statements of witnesses should be taken while their memories are fresh. Even if you have been seriously injured, the initial work needs to be done as soon as possible, and a relative can start your claim off if they have your written authority.

It is *your* claim and you must take responsibility for it. You cannot expect to simply give your solicitor initial instructions and then sit back and wait for your settlement cheque. You must provide wage slips and P60s if you have a loss of earnings claim, or audited accounts if you are self-employed. You may have to undergo medical examinations and obtain quotes for domestic or gardening assistance. You must provide receipts for expenses, and bus and rail tickets if you have had to use public transport.

I recommend that you keep a diary of all matters relating to your claim, so that you have a record of visits to doctors and hospital, of when your car was collected from the repairer, and of all journeys involving expense which you would not have incurred if there had not been an accident. Your solicitor will need these details to set out your claim accurately, and to compile a statement of your evidence.

Make your instructions to your solicitor clear and

precise. Much delay is caused by clients giving vague, ambiguous or conflicting information about their employment and damaged property, or by failing to respond to their solicitor's requests for information. Tell your solicitor everything which might possibly be relevant to your claim. Do not keep back things which you think might be unhelpful to your claim. Your opponent will probe deeply into all matters, looking for weaknesses in your claim. If your opponent discovers something about you, such as an earlier accident or that you left your job for reasons other than your injury, your solicitor could be taken by surprise. Early disclosure of these details to your solicitor will give him a chance to consider how to minimize their effect. If the information comes to light close to the date of the trial, or even at the trial itself, it could have disastrous consequences for your claim.

## Counsel

Your solicitor may seek the advice of a barrister, who will be referred to as 'counsel' by lawyers. Their full title is barrister at law. Barristers practise on their own, although they group together in offices known as chambers to share expenses and conference facilities, and to attract instructions from solicitors. It is a rule of the General Council of the Bar, which supervises barristers, that they cannot accept instructions directly from members of the public. Barristers specialize in presenting cases in court, in advising on the strength and sufficiency of evidence, and in writing second opinions on the value of a claim. A conference with counsel might be arranged, where the strengths and weaknesses of the evidence can be discussed with you and a completely fresh and objective view of your prospects at trial can be obtained.

After obtaining their degree, student barristers join one of the Inns of Court. These Inns, Lincoln's Inn, Gray's Inn, Middle Temple and Inner Temple, were formerly lodgings for barristers. They now have a role of governing, educating and disciplining barristers, and also as their club. The students take a further course, the Bar examinations, and become barristers on being 'called to the bar' by their Inn. The bar was a barrier in the well of the court keeping the public away from the judges. Advocates could address the judges from the bar. The term 'Bar' is now a collective term for all barristers. The new barrister must then assist a practising barrister as his pupil for one year before he can accept instructions in a case from a solicitor.

Some barristers apply for the title of Queen's Counsel. A QC, who is also known as a 'silk' from his court robe, and sometimes 'Leading Counsel', must have at least ten years experience of appearing in the higher courts. A barrister who is not a QC is called a Junior Counsel, even though he may have decades of experience. Some barristers do not seek appointment to QC. The title of QC, although conferring prestige, can result in a drop in income to particularly successful juniors because the higher fees which QCs expect to charge may result in a reduction in the number of new instructions. Your solicitor will not recommend that a QC should be instructed in your case, because of the high cost, unless there is a compelling reason to do so. It might be that a particular barrister with specialist knowledge and experience required for your case happens to be a QC. If you are funding your own case, you can of course choose to have your solicitor instruct any barrister you choose, including a QC. However, you may not recover all of a QC's fee from the other side even if you win your case. Solicitors can also now apply for appointment to QC.

## Litigant in person

You may wish to run your claim yourself, including presenting it in court. You have an automatic right to be heard by the court in your own case. In the county court small claims procedure you can have someone who is not a lawyer present your case for you. However, there are many pitfalls. You will not have the benefit of the objective opinion of your case of an experienced lawyer. Righteous indignation, and inexperience of litigation, can blind a person to the weaknesses in his case.

Of equal concern are the procedural difficulties. You must comply with all of the rules concerning correct service of proceedings, accuracy of pleadings, serving the list of documents and exchanging witness statements within the timetable set by the rules. In particular, you may find that your claim has been struck out because you have missed a deadline. The most common errors are being late in serving proceedings and in applying for a hearing date.

# 14 FUNDING YOUR CLAIM –

## WHAT IT WILL COST AND HOW TO AFFORD IT

Pursuing your claim will not be cheap. Leaving aside the cost of instructing a solicitor and barrister, there are likely to be expenses which you must pay as your claim progresses.

Here are some examples:

| | |
|---|---|
| Police accident report | £ 45 |
| Medical report | £100 |
| Hospital administration fee to release what may be a one-page attendance sheet | £ 10 |
| X-rays | £ 75 |
| Fee for release of your doctor's notes | £ 10 |
| Court fee for issue of summons, up to | £ 80 |
| High Court fee for issue of writ | £120 |

There may also be fees for an accountant's report, employment consultant's report, further medical reports. Much of this cost will be recovered from the other side if your claim is successful, but because a claim can take well over three years to settle, funding it can be very difficult.

### Legal Aid

The Legal Aid Board is funded by the Government to provide financial support for obtaining legal advice and assistance. There are two tests which must be satisfied if Legal Aid funding is to be granted for legal assistance. Only the first test, the means test, applies if you are seeking just legal advice. This is called the Green Form scheme, and you can obtain up to two hours worth of advice from a solicitor, although he cannot take any steps to progress your claim. You would need to pass both tests to be granted a Legal Aid certificate before he could do that. The tests are:

1 Your disposable income, capital and savings must not be more than the prescribed limits. These eligibility limits for a Legal Aid certificate at May 1995 are:

  Capital (the value of your assets and savings) of £3,000 if you have no dependants. You can have a little more capital and still be eligible if you have dependants. The part of the value of the house you live in which would be yours if it was sold, which is called the equity, and also your furniture, is not counted.

  Disposable income of £64 per week. If your disposable income is more than this but not more than £156 per week, you are still eligible, but you must pay a contribution. Disposable income is calculated by deducting from your weekly income from all sources:

  - i Income tax and National Insurance contributions.
  - ii Housing costs such as rent or mortgage repayments, council tax, water and power.
  - iii £26.50 for a partner, or the actual maintenance sum paid by you if you are separated or divorced.
  - iv Sums received by you as disability living allowance or attendance allowance.
  - v £15.95 for each dependant child under eleven, £23.40 if aged eleven to seventeen, £36.80 if over eighteen.

  In calculating your income, your partner's means are taken into account. The capital limit for Green Form advice is only £1,535 even with two dependants, and the disposable income limit is £72 per week. There is no contribution scheme for people with incomes above that figure. You can check with any solicitor who operates the Legal Aid scheme whether you will qualify under the financial test. He will not charge you for this. A child is entitled to Legal Aid in his own right, and most children will pass the financial test.

In response to concern about people with an apparently wealthy lifestyle being granted Legal Aid, the government proposes to tighten the assessment procedure. The proposals include a limit of £100,000 on each of the amount of equity and mortgage relating to an applicant's home which is to be disregarded when assessing an applicant's capital. Repayments in respect of the amount of mortgage above £100,000 will be classed as disposable income.

First example: If an applicant has a house worth £150,000 and no mortgage, he will be assessed as having £50,000 of his equity of £150,000 as available capital.

Second example: If his house is worth £250,000 with a mortgage of £150,000, only £100,000 of his mortgage will be disregarded. This leaves £150,000 which would be regarded as equity. Of this, only £100,000 would be disregarded. The final £50,000 would be considered as available capital. In addition, any repayments of the mortgage loan over £100,000 would not be deducted from total income when calculating the disposable income. In this second example, the repayments in respect of £50,000 of the full mortgage loan of £150,000 would be included in disposable income.

A special investigation unit is also to be set up to inquire further into complex cases.

In particular, where an applicant claims to have little money but is supported in an apparently wealthy style by others, there will be a discretion to take the value of these advantages into account.

2 If you pass the financial test, you must then pass the merits test. Your claim must have reasonable prospects of success, and be of a sufficient value, usually not less than £1,000. A general test is whether a prudent person of moderate means would be prepared to fund the claim himself, having been advised that his chances of success are better than even. If the answer which suggests itself is 'yes', then the claim is likely to be considered to have sufficient merit to be supported by Legal Aid, and a Legal Aid certificate can be granted. This authorizes your solicitor to take specified steps in progressing your claim, in the knowledge that he will be paid his reasonable costs by the Legal Aid Board if he cannot get those costs from the other driver or his insurer. The decision on whether your claim should be supported is made by the Legal Aid Board. It is possible to appeal against a refusal of support.

When making an application for Legal Aid, there are two forms to complete. The application form CLA1 is of eight pages. Your solicitor may help you with this, as a statement of your claim is required, and it needs to have enough detail to give the Legal Aid Board a reasonable idea of the merits and value of your claim. You must also complete a financial circumstances form CLA4A of twelve pages. From the details you give on this form, your solicitor should be able to tell you if you have passed the financial test.

He will not be able to tell you if you have passed the merits test, as this is a matter for the Legal Aid Board. This may change soon. Some solicitors firms have a franchise from the Legal Aid Board. A franchised firm must have administrative systems approved and monitored by the Board. These firms may be authorized to grant Legal Aid on behalf of the Board in the future. Your solicitor should be able to tell you if your claim has a realistic prospect of success, although he is unlikely to have very much evidence to go on at that stage.

You must tell the Legal Aid Board of any changes in your circumstances which may affect your claim or your entitlement to a certificate. The Legal Aid Board can end its support, by discharging the certificate, if matters come to light which indicate that your case is weaker than was originally thought. The Legal Aid Board can also revoke a certificate, which withdraws support going back to the start of the claim. You would then become liable for all legal costs incurred, if you knew that the information you have given to the Legal Aid Board or your solicitor is untrue.

Legal Aid is a form of interest-free loan. If you are successful with your claim, you must repay the Legal Aid Board's outlay. Since you should recover most of your costs from the other side, this will not usually affect the sum which you eventually receive too much. If your claim fails, Legal Aid will pay your solicitor and the necessary expenses. It will not pay the other side's costs, but they cannot recover their costs from you if you were assisted by Legal Aid except in very exceptional circumstances.

## Legal costs insurance

Your motor insurance broker may offer you legal costs insurance. The premium for this is typically about £15 extra. You might have this valuable insurance cover without knowing it, as it is sometimes an additional benefit of the insurance policy, like windscreen cover. Check your insurance documents carefully, or check with your broker, to see if you have this cover. I strongly recommend it. This cover is sometimes available as an extension of household insurance.

If you suffer losses caused by a road accident, your legal costs insurer will advise you what to do. They may attempt to recover your losses themselves, particularly where liability is not disputed and your losses are straightforward such as only repairs and policy excess, or they will pass your claim to an approved firm of solicitors. You may choose your own solicitor, but your legal costs insurer will need to be satisfied that he is experienced in handling road accident claims.

The solicitor appointed to deal with your claim will not ask you for any costs for the necessary steps and expenses. If you are successful with your claim, his costs will be paid by your opponent. If you are not successful, or where your opponent is entitled to some of his costs, all costs will be paid by your legal costs insurer. However, if you abandon your claim without good reason, and no costs can be recovered from your opponent, your legal costs insurer may look to you to reimburse their outlay.

Like all insurance, there is a limit to the risk which your legal costs insurer will accept. If you insist on pursuing your claim against the advice of your solicitor, your legal costs insurer may decline to support your claim any further. This may happen if your opponent makes a payment into court. If you reject the sum paid into court, which is an offer to settle your claim in that sum, but you do not obtain a better sum at trial, you are responsible for the costs of both sides from the date twenty-one days after the money was paid into court. This would mean your legal costs insurer would have to settle a substantial legal bill even though you won your case. This is because, as it turned out, the payment into court was an adequate sum, and your opponent should not have to pay his own costs or yours because you did not think it was adequate.

Your solicitor has a duty to your legal costs insurer as well as to you. He must advise them if you reject a payment into court which he thinks is a realistic sum. Where there is a real risk that the payment into court would not be beaten at trial, further financial support is likely to be refused. You could still continue with your claim, but you would have to accept the risk of having to pay substantial legal costs yourself if you do not beat the payment into court.

## Conditional fees

Under this arrangement, your solicitor will agree to take your case, but you will not have to pay him any costs in advance. However, he may require you to pay for the cost of medical and other reports or disbursements, and court fees. If you win your case, you will pay your solicitor at a higher rate than normal, which will be agreed in advance. This additional charge is to compensate your solicitor for the risk of not being paid if you lose your case. You cannot recover this uplift from your opponent, since he is not responsible for how you fund your claim, and this extra money will come out of your compensation.

If you lose your case, or you cannot recover your costs from the other side for some other reason, you will not have to pay your solicitor for his time. It will be necessary to have some form of insurance arranged to protect you from your opponent's claim for his costs. You will therefore need to have at least the money to pay this insurance premium, likely to be about £100, before you can begin your claim.

## Trade Unions

If you are a member of a trade union, ask your representative about the possibility of union support for your claim. While full financial support may only be available for industrial accident and disease cases, your union might be able to help you with advice and some financial assistance.

## Private funding

If you have to fund your claim yourself, you will have to pay for disbursements such as medical reports as they arise. You will also have to pay your solicitor for his time as the case progresses. He will send to you interim bills setting out what has been done and the cost due. At the conclusion of your claim he will send you a final bill. Sums paid on interim bills will be deducted and he will tell you how much of your costs he has been able to get back from your opponent, which could mean a refund of much of what you have had to pay. If you abandon your claim for any reason, you cannot get your costs from your opponent and you may have to pay his costs.

If you win your case, it is usual for your opponent to pay your costs. The amount of costs which he is ordered to pay may be less than your solicitor's bill. You are responsible for paying this, so it will reduce the amount of your compensation.

## Why do solicitors cost so much?

Solicitors are no more expensive than other professional people such as doctors, accountants, architects and barristers. Solicitors usually charge for their work according to the time spent on it. There is a basic charge-out rate, reflecting the cost of doing the work. This represents a proportion of the overhead costs allocated to each case. These overheads, while including the usual business expenses of premises, staff salaries, office equipment and stationery, also include the following expenses of a legal practice:

Practising certificate, almost £500 for each solicitor.

Books, journals, computer software and subscriptions to case data-bases to keep up to date with the rapidly changing law and procedures. Many firms find it necessary to employ a librarian to manage the huge volume of information which must be available to solicitors.

Training. All solicitors must complete a minimum of sixteen hours attendance each year on approved courses. A typical budget is £500 for each solicitor. Many firms find it necessary to employ a training officer.

Negligence insurance premium. This is typically a very high sum indeed. It provides clients with a guarantee of compensation if they suffer loss due to their solicitor's fault. While you will have little sympathy for a solicitor who makes a mistake, in many cases the act complained of is ruled to have been a mistake only at a later date. Today's work is judged by tomorrow's standards if the complaint goes to trial. Standards and expectations are rising. The courts are constantly changing the law, and some legislation has a retrospective effect. A percentage of the charge-out rate is added to provide a profit.

If you are going to be responsible for paying your solicitor his fee, ask him to explain his charging structure at the first interview. However, it will not be possible to tell you what the total cost is likely to be. The amount of work required on your case will depend on many factors such as whether your opponent disputes your claim, what evidence is needed to prove it, and whether your case goes to trial.

# 15 RECOVERING YOUR COSTS

If you fund your claim yourself, or you are making a contribution to your Legal Aid, you will be particularly interested in recovering your costs. If you are successful with your claim, you can usually recover from the other side those costs which you have incurred which were reasonable and necessary to progress your claim. The court has a discretion to refuse to award you your costs, although this would be unusual. You cannot get your costs if your opponent has Legal Aid.

You will not recover the cost of a medical report which you do not agree with and which you do not want your opponent to see. Also, you will not recover the cost of your solicitor sending you reminder letters because you have not replied to earlier letters requesting information. That is no concern of your opponent, and he cannot be made to pay for it.

## Small claims

If your claim is not likely to be worth more than £1,000 for injury, £3000 if no injury, there is a restriction on the costs you can get back. For instance, if your claim is for car repairs costing £1500 and loss of use of your car for two weeks, you can only expect to recover about £1600, and so it is a 'small claim'. Another example is of a minor whiplash injury which settles down after a few weeks, so that your claim might be worth about £700. If your claim is a small claim, you will get back the cost of your reasonable disbursements, the court fees for issuing the summons and applying for a hearing date, the reasonable expenses of you and your witnesses attending court, and a small sum towards your solicitor's fee if you have instructed him to prepare the summons. You will not get back the cost of any other work done for you by your solicitor such as presenting your case in court.

## Taxation

You will have a contractual relationship with your solicitor, and you are responsible for paying his fee and expenses. He will try to recover as much of this sum as he can from your opponent. If costs cannot be agreed with your opponent, your solicitor's bill will be reviewed by a judge in a procedure known as taxation of costs. The taxing judge may reduce the bill payable by your opponent, and so you will be responsible for paying to your solicitor the sum which was 'taxed off' of the bill.

The county court rules set out scales of costs which a winning litigant will be allowed to recover from his opponent. They are very unrealistic and you will have had to pay very much more for the service. For example, the rules prescribe £70 for counsel's opinion on quantum, but counsel's fee is likely to be in the bracket £125-£200. Higher sums are allowed in the High Court. The taxing judge has a discretion to allow more than the prescribed rates.

## Your legal costs

Your solicitor cannot tell you in advance how much it will cost to take your claim to a conclusion. This is because he cannot predict how your opponent will react to your claim. He might accept liability straight away, and even make an early and realistic offer to settle your claim. On the other hand, he might oppose you at every stage all the way to trial. As well as your own legal costs, you will be responsible for your opponents taxed costs if you are not successful with your claim.

## Remuneration certificate

If you think that your solicitor's bill is too high, you can ask him to obtain a remuneration certificate from the Law Society. An officer of the Law Society will review the file and certify what he considers to be a fair sum due to the solicitor in the particular circumstances. If this is less than your solicitor's bill, you need only pay the sum on the certificate. If you ask your solicitor to send for a remuneration certificate, you must first pay half of his fee and all of the VAT and expenses on the bill.

If you are still not satisfied, you can apply to have the bill taxed by the court. Unless the bill is reduced by at least 20% on taxation, you will have to pay the costs of this procedure.

Once you have settled your solicitor's bill, you are entitled to possession of your file if you want it, since it belongs to you. Your solicitor will archive the file for a period of six years at no charge and then destroy it unless you ask for it. He will not charge you for retrieving the file from storage, but may ask for the postage cost in advance.

## Litigant in person

If you run a claim successfully yourself, you can ask for the cost of your time in doing the work. You cannot claim at the same rate that a solicitor would charge, since you would of course take very much longer to do work on your case of the type which a solicitor is likely to do every day. If you have spent time on your case which you would otherwise have been paid for, you can claim a reasonable time at your normal earning rate. This is subject to a maximum of two thirds of what the court would allow a solicitor to charge for the same work. If you have spent only your spare time in doing the work on your case, you can claim a reasonable time at a fixed rate, currently £8.25 per hour. In the small claims procedure, you can have anyone of your choice to speak for you. If your non-lawyer representative charges you a fee for advising and representing you, this is not recoverable from your opponent.

# 16 VALUING YOUR CLAIM

Liability is about who must pay compensation. Quantum (of damages) is about how much is to be paid. In chapters 7 and 8 on what to claim for, I explained the difference between special damages and general damages. This chapter deals with how a value is found for the various heads of claim.

## Property damage

*Loss of use of your car*
This is an item of general damages, in that the value of the loss cannot be established by receipts or estimates. It is the value which the court puts on this disadvantage which has been caused by the accident. The awards made by the courts in similar cases are put forward to the other side in negotiations as a basis for settlement of this head of claim.

While your car is undrivable and awaiting repair, and while it is being repaired, you are deprived of the use of it. It does not matter that you had no particular journeys to make, or even that your car was usually used by someone else, you are still deprived of the option of using it. If you hire a car, you then have a substitute car and so are not deprived of the use of one.

You will recover loss of use for a reasonable period. What this period is depends on your particular circumstances. It may be that you cannot afford to have your car repaired or replaced. If the other driver continues to deny liability, you might recover for loss of use right up to the date you receive compensation for repairs or the pre-accident value of your car. Once you are paid your car's value by your own insurer under a comprehensive policy, your claim for loss of use will run from the date of the accident until about fourteen days after receipt of your own insurer's settlement cheque. This should be enough time to find a replacement car.

The rate of compensation for loss of use varies widely, depending on the views of particular judges. The range is usually between £35 and £75 per week. The factors which a judge will take into consideration include the availability of alternative transport. A person living in a remote rural area is more dependent on their car than is a person in a city with access to public transport. However, particularly if you are a woman, it is not reasonable to expect you to use public transport at night.

### *Special damages*

These are expenses or other financial loss which can be valued by means of receipts, price lists or expert valuation.

*Your car*

If it is worth having the car repaired, the sum recoverable is the cheaper of at least two estimates. If it is uneconomical to repair the car, it will be written off as a total loss except for what it will fetch as scrap. The quantum is the pre-accident value of your car net of its scrap value. This is established by having it inspected by a motor vehicle assessor and by reference to the published car price guides such as *Parker's,* or by comparison with similar models in similar condition offered for sale in newspapers. The pre-accident value of the car takes no account of what you paid for it, or how much you have spent on it, or how much you loved it, or how much it will cost to buy another car. Most people are disappointed with the pre-accident value figure.

*Clothing and other personal possessions*

These are valued at either their cost price, as

established by receipts, or at their replacement cost less a deduction for the period of use.

## Injury and associated losses

The possible heads of general damages, being those which are not direct financial losses but which ought to attract compensation, include those listed in chapter 8. A loss of promotion prospects is often difficult to establish. You may have an optimistic expectation of your prospects of advancement in your job. Employers are often unable, or unwilling, to state that you were or were not in line for promotion. If you are fortunate enough to have an employer willing to commit himself on this matter, the loss is your disappointment. Its value depends on when you might regain the prospect of advancement. There is also a potential loss of earnings if the promotion would have meant an increase in your pay. The figures can be obtained from your employer, or from someone who is already in the higher position if they are willing to assist you.

Loss of congenial employment and loss of holiday enjoyment are subjective matters and are valued according to the degree of importance their loss is to you. You should set this out fully in your witness statement. For instance, if the holiday was to have been your honeymoon, the loss is likely to be particularly important to you.

The value of a disability on the labour market is assessed more objectively. It is not that you think your employability is reduced which counts, but what a potential employer is likely to think. Awards made in past cases can help. It is usually quite modest but can, in exceptional cases, be as high as £20,000.

Putting a value on an injury is never easy. You are entitled to be compensated for your injury, as far as money can do it. The different effect of the same injury on different people can be immense, and this will be taken into account by the court. However, there has to be a starting-point. This is found in the decisions of courts in reported cases which dealt with a similar injury. Some of these cases are collected together and published in the legal press as a guide to lawyers. Also, a general guide has been published, a form of 'tariff', of ranges of likely award for various types of injury. This sets out quite wide scales of monetary award for particular types of injury. In suggesting a likely range of awards I have taken these guidelines into account, but I have relied particularly on reports of awards made at trial.

I must stress that my suggested figures are no more than a starting-point, set out here to give you at least a clue to part of the answer to one of the questions you most want answered – 'How much will I get?' There are very many factors which can persuade the judge that a higher or lower award is appropriate in a particular case. Some of them are objective, likely to affect most people suffering from a particular injury. Others may be subjective, in that you suffer more than most people would because of your individual circumstances. It does not matter that you have a special vulnerability which means that the effect of a particular injury on you is worse than might be expected. This is called an 'eggshell skull' case. The analogy is with someone who is struck a moderate blow on the head which would not fracture a normal skull. If the victim has a thin skull, an 'eggshell' skull, and suffers unexpectedly severe injury as a result, the person causing the injury is liable for the full effect of it even though it was not foreseen.

The importance of a satisfactory sex life is recognized by society and is now openly discussed. You may have an understandable reluctance to put forward details of any loss to this part of your life. However, it can lead to marital disharmony and family break-up, and it is taken seriously by the courts.

Here are some examples of types of injury and the likely ranges of award. The medical terms are those which appear in the case reports and will have been taken from the medical evidence given at trial. You will be able to find the meaning of many of them in the glossary of medical terms. At the end of the case reports, I have added an adjusted compensation figure for 1995 which takes account of inflation since the date of the original award. It is for you, with the assistance of your legal advisers, to establish where on the scale of severity your injury falls.

*Catastrophic injury*

This category, which would include amputation, paralysis, complete loss of sight and brain damage, is of such severity that the claimant is unable to care for himself. Although very substantial sums are often awarded in these cases, they are global settlements and include sums for special equipment, for loss of future earnings and for the cost of future nursing care. The starting point in considering awards for pain, suffering and loss of amenity will be in the region of £100,000.

*Frith* v. *Blaylock* (High Court 1994). The plaintiff was involved in a road accident while driving a lorry in 1987. He was aged twenty-five. He suffered fractures to his T12 and L1 vertebrae with resulting paraplegia. He also sustained multiple fractures to one arm and both legs. He is confined to a wheelchair. The award was £80,000 but, the case report says, reduced by 30% for contributory negligence.

*Head injury*

Where this results in a substantial reduction in memory, intellectual ability, powers of concentration, and in increased aggression and irritability, the likely award will be in the bracket £20,000–£50,000.

For a less severe head injury, where treatment is likely to be effective and there is a realistic expectation of improvement, the range is £5,000–£15,000. Where the injury results in headaches only, the range of award is £1,000–£6,000. Severe migraine-like headaches persisting for more than three years attract awards at the top end of the bracket.

*Matthews* v. *Oldfield* (High Court 1991). A car driver sustained a head injury which needed three stitches. He suffered from headaches for about eighteen months. Award: £4,500 (£5,100 in 1995).

*Loss or impairment of senses*
I have included total loss of sight in the catastrophic injuries category. Severe partial loss of sight will attract an award in the region of £20,000. Loss or serious impairment of taste or smell will be valued at about £8,000. There are follow-on effects of this type of loss which can be dangerous, such as being unable to detect toxic fumes. This and other factors such as the effect of the loss of the sense of smell to a keen flower grower would be likely to increase the award. Moderate but permanent partial hearing loss and tinnitus should each attract about £10,000.

*Wood* v. *Cleaver* (Birkenhead county court 1993). A man aged thirty-four was knocked off his bicycle by a car in 1991. He suffered a fractured skull and was in hospital for eight days. He suffered bouts of dizziness and his senses of taste and smell were much impaired. Award: £10,000 (£10,800 in 1995).

*Bettany* v. *Harvey Plant* (Leicester county court 1993). Immediately following a road accident in 1990, a man aged forty-nine developed tinnitus, a loud constant hissing, in both ears. It was moderate to severe and caused sleep disturbance, and there was minor loss of hearing. It was likely to be permanent. Award £12,500 (£13,500 in 1995).

*Facial injury*
A broken nose can range from a crack to a serious

injury requiring several operations. The effect of a displaced nose fracture which results in disfigurement might be thought to be more serious to a young woman, and an award higher than the usual range of £1,000-£8,000 could be appropriate. If teeth are knocked out or are damaged to the extent that they need to be taken out, the award is about £500 for a back tooth and £1,000 for a front tooth.

*Shaw* v. *Gralette* (Croydon county court 1994). A woman motorcyclist was in collision with a cyclist and she suffered a displaced fractured nose. This was successfully operated on some fifteen months after the accident because of breathing difficulties. She had other minor injuries and nervousness when travelling by motorcycle. Award: £2,250 (£2,360 in 1995).

*Neck and back*

Soft tissue injuries to neck and back are very common in road accidents. They usually result from the sudden reversal of the body's direction of travel when the car is hit from behind or is brought to a sudden stop by a front-end collision. It is called a whiplash injury, and can result in the straining of the muscles, ligaments and tendons of the neck, shoulders and back. Other common injuries are chipped or fractured vertebrae, slipped disc where the spongy cushion between the vertebrae is displaced, and disruption of the nerves in the spine.

A very severe and permanent neck or back injury will be valued at about £50,000, with a lesser injury involving a fracture or dislocation, or severe irreparable soft tissue damage attracting £15,000.

A moderately severe injury such as whiplash where the pain and limitation of movement are permanent would be awarded up to £10,000. With a less severe injury where the symptoms are permanent but fairly minor, the likely sum is about £5,000.

*Vater* v. *Dry Silver (in Liquidation)* (Pontypridd county court 1993). A woman aged thirty-five suffered a neck whiplash injury in a road accident in 1986. She wore a support collar for six months and underwent physiotherapy treatment. She has continuing symptoms which restrict her activities with housework and gardening and she had to change her job to a less active one. Flexion and extension of her neck are restricted to about half of the normal range. Award: £9,500 (£10,750 in 1995).

*Hamer* v. *North West Water Authority* (Burnley county court 1992). A bus driver aged thirty-six suffered a jarring injury to his back when his bus went over a depression in the road in 1985. He had severe lower back pain with limited movement, and the discomfort radiated down both of his legs. He could not run, and he could walk for only five minutes. He had to avoid bending, lifting and carrying. He had a pre-existing degenerative condition in his back which had not troubled him very much. The accident had made his back condition worse. It brought the extra pain and discomfort forward by five years. He also suffered stiffness and creaking in his neck. Total award for the injuries: £7,000 (£7,900 in 1995).

*Arms and legs*

For a severe fracture requiring repair with screws and wires, but where a reasonable recovery is likely, expect about £15,000. Simple fractures which unite well without residual weakness attract about £3,000.

*Ford* v. *Large* (CA 1992). A woman of twenty-one suffered an injury to her dominant wrist in a road accident in 1988. It was a fracture to the distal radius with some comminution but with minimal displacement. The radius was slightly shortened and there was a fracture to the tip of the ulna. Her wrist was in plaster for five weeks. She was left with periodic clicking and aching, crepitus and a reduction in flexion and grip. Award: £6,500 (£8,840 in 1995).

*Frost* v. *Palmer* (CA 1993). Man aged thirty-one suffered multiple fractures of his lower leg and knee in a road accident in 1984. He underwent ten operations which saved his leg although it was shortened and disfigured and his knee was unstable and with restricted movement. He suffered a reactive depression, and osteoarthritis would set in later. He was awarded £28,000 (£31,900 in 1995).

*Knee injury*
The knee is vulnerable to damage to the ligaments which keep the joint stable and free-moving. A serious injury resulting in a need for considerable treatment and a permanently painful and unstable joint could be valued at £25,000. Where the knee is usable but aches after activity, the award would be unlikely to exceed £8,000.

*Tilson* v. *Taylor* (High Court 1993). A man of thirty-nine was driving on a main road in 1988 when the defendant drove from a side road causing a collision. The plaintiff banged his knee which later swelled up. Blood was drained from it and he had physiotherapy. An arthroscopy showed damaged and loose cartilage and an MRI scan confirmed the need for a tibial osteotomy. Knee joint replacements would be required in the future. His knee is unstable and he wears a brace. He controls the pain with analgesics. Award £25,000 (£27,500 in 1995).

*Fractured fingers and toes*
The level of award depends on remaining gripping power in respect of fingers and any residual limping in respect of toes, and is generally up to £3,000.

*Psychological injury*

This can range from severe post-traumatic stress disorder, through depression to mild anxiety when travelling in a car. It is for a psychiatrist to identify the type and extent of any psychiatric injury by isolating the reaction caused by the accident or the resulting injury from the other effects which result from the stresses of life. The possible need for a psychiatric assessment can be measured by the extent to which you are still troubled by thoughts of the accident, whether (A) not at all, (B) rarely, (C) sometimes or (D) often. Try answering the following questions and allocate nil points for A, one point for B, two points for C and five points for D. A total score of more than twenty may indicate the presence of a stress disorder:

1 You thought about it unintentionally.

2 You avoided letting yourself get upset when you thought about it or were reminded of it.

3 You tried to remove it from your memory.

4 You had trouble falling or staying asleep because thoughts or pictures of it came into your mind.

5 You had waves of strong feelings about it.

6 You dreamt about it.

7 You avoided anything which reminded you of it.

8 You felt as though it had not happened, it was not real.

9 You avoided talking about it.

Severe post-traumatic stress disorder can render the sufferer incapable of living a normal life. In these cases, an award could be in the region of £30,000. More usually, the effects of the disorder cause flashbacks and intrusive thoughts which are distressing but not disabling. The award in these cases, depending on the response to treatment, is likely to be in the region of £5,000.

*Minor injuries*
These are often more difficult to value than are more serious injuries. The definition 'minor' is also rather subjective. An example is *Hutchins* v. *Jackson* (Bournemouth county court 1994). The plaintiff was thrown from his motorcycle in the accident and suffered a deep laceration to the little finger of his non-dominant hand. He had three stitches, a tetanus injection and took analgesics. The wound had healed after five months. The judge described the injury as 'minor but not trivial'. Award: £750.

Whiplash is a very common injury resulting from even quite minor collisions:

*Rothwell* v. *Hodson* (Horsham county court 1994). A woman of nineteen suffered a whiplash injury to her neck and lower back in a road accident in 1991. The symptoms settled after six months but returned after she did some heavy lifting. The evidence was that her symptoms were likely to disappear within a few years. Award: £4,750.

Included in a particular award is a sum intended to compensate for loss of amenity. This loss depends on the effect of the injury on the claimant's life, and takes into account his age, previous health, pre-accident hobbies, sporting and other interests and realistic expectations for the future if these have been affected by the injury.

If you have suffered multiple injuries, you do not add together the likely awards for the individual injuries. This is because of the overlap effect of more than one injury. Imagine that you are suffering pain and discomfort from, for example, a broken leg. The level of additional pain and discomfort, and the effect on your quality of life, contributed by also having a broken wrist, is considered to be less than the individual injuries at different times. In the same way, if you have a broken leg, your mobility is impaired. The impairment is not much greater if you have broken both legs. You might not think this is fair. You will find a discussion of fairness, justice and the legal system at chapter 26.

Even when your solicitor has considered all the factors affecting your claim, and he has suggested what he thinks your claim is worth, he cannot tell you with any certainty what sum of money you will receive as compensation for your injury. If your case goes to court, the judge will make an award to the extent that you prove your case to his satisfaction. There are many factors which affect this, such as the impression you and your witnesses make, and also the performance of your opponent and his witnesses. There are sometimes surprises at trial, with awards being unexpectedly generous or disappointingly low. Out-of-court settlements are arrived at by considering what a judge might award at trial in the particular circumstances.

Whatever you achieve is likely to be less than you deserve. It is recognized that compensation awards by English and Scottish courts for personal injury are low. The Law Commission, in its report No. 225 *Personal Injury Compensation: How Much is Enough?* published by HMSO in October 1994, noted the inadequacy of current awards of damages in many cases. At present, judges who make substantially higher awards than have been made in past cases, allowing for inflation, might see their awards overturned on appeal.

Your opponent's insurer is entitled to have you examined by medical specialists of their own choosing, and also to see your full medical records. They might also instruct an agent to take video footage of you without you being aware of it. This is legitimate, and is intended to demonstrate that you are not as disabled as you say you are, and as the medical evidence would indicate.

If you have a medical condition which you had before the accident, such as wear and degeneration in your spine, or the effects of an earlier accident, and this is likely to be contributing to your pain and loss of amenity, this will have the effect of reducing the value of your claim.

## Disability on the labour market

This is sometimes called a *Smith* v. *Manchester* award (when citing civil cases say, as here, Smith *and* Manchester) from a leading case on this head of claim in 1974. Mrs Smith worked in a nursing home run by Manchester Corporation. She slipped on a wet floor and suffered an injury, but she was able to return to work. She suffered continuing symptoms from her injury which meant that she could only perform light duties. Her employer, Manchester Corporation, was a considerate employer and assured her that it would try to ensure that her employment would continue. Even so, it was held that, should Mrs Smith ever find herself looking for another job for some reason, she would be less employable than she was before her accident.

The value of a *Smith* v. *Manchester* award depends on factors such as the likely level of competition in the range of occupations open to the claimant, and age (a claimant nearing retirement will receive a very modest award, if any). The range of awards is typically £500 to £15,000.

### *Special damages*

*Loss of earnings*

You can recover what you have lost in earnings after deduction of tax and National Insurance. Lost overtime earnings, bonus or commission payments are also recoverable. You must prove these losses by showing a history of receiving them, and that these payments are likely to have continued during the period when you were unable to work because of the accident.

Pay slips, certificates of pay, income tax and national insurance contributions (form P60) and a record of earnings for at least three months before the accident are usually required. Any increases paid to your colleagues should be taken into account. Your employer may have paid you in full under a contractual sick pay scheme which requires you to repay it if you receive compensation. Your sick pay might include Statutory Sick Pay and this element could be deducted from your settlement sum under the rules discussed in chapter 19. Sums equivalent to both of these deductions need to be claimed so as to offset the deductions.

If you have spent more than about a week in hospital because of the accident, your opponent can make a reduction in the compensation for lost income. This is because you have been kept at public expense and so made a saving in your living costs.

*Spouse's loss of earnings*

If your spouse (which here can mean spouse, parent or adult child) has stayed at home to look after you, and lost earnings because of it, you cannot claim for that loss as such. What you can claim for is the reasonable cost of nursing care, and your spouse's loss of earnings may be allowed if it is not more than the cost of alternative care.

It does not matter that the carer does not expect to be paid. If your spouse was not working, or continues to work as well as taking care of you, you can still claim a reasonable sum to represent the cost of engaging someone to nurse you, less a discount to take account of tasks which a spouse would be likely to do before your accident. If you need professional nursing care, the reasonable cost of this can be claimed. Any claim for nursing care must be supported by medical advice.

## Future earnings

If it appears likely that you will not be able to return to work because of your injury, or that you can only do work which pays less than you were earning previously, you should claim for a loss of future earnings. A figure is calculated for your likely earnings in your pre-accident employment for the years up to normal retirement age for that job. Possible increases in pay are taken into account, as are deductions of tax and National Insurance. From this sum is deducted any likely future earnings such as from a job you can manage with your injury.

A further reduction is also likely, to take account of the risks of unemployment, injury from other causes or early death which you would have faced anyway. The other driver is not required to provide you with a guaranteed income which was not guaranteed before the accident. A reduction will also be made to take account of you receiving future earnings as a lump sum now, rather than spread over the period you would have worked.

## Self-employed

If you were self-employed, your claim for loss of profits will need some documentary evidence to support it. The usual requirement is audited accounts for at least three years before the accident, and possibly also tax assessments. You will have some difficulty if your business is newly established, because you will not have a track record of profitability on which to base your claim. If you are a director of a company and a substantial shareholder, you may be able to claim for a loss of profits of the company in proportion to your loss as shareholder. The directorship would need to be your only or main occupation.

## Loss of pension

If you belonged to a company pension scheme, you may have lost pension benefits. These may be all, or part, of a lump sum and pension income which you would have received if you had worked until the normal retirement age for your job. Your claim would be for the part of any lump sum which you have lost due to early retirement, and for a sum sufficient to buy an annuity which is likely to provide the lost pension income.

If you receive a pension as a result of having to take early retirement due to your injury, this is disregarded and will not reduce your award. If you are claiming loss of dependency following the death of a spouse or someone else who supported you financially, any pension and life assurance benefit is also disregarded. Your opponent cannot take advantage of these prudent arrangements.

# 17 SETTLING BY NEGOTIATION

## Negotiating

Your Solicitor will try to negotiate a settlement of your claim with the other driver's insurer or their solicitors. He will inform you of any offer they make to settle your claim, and advise you on whether or not he thinks it is a realistic offer compared with what you might reasonably expect to get at trial. Negotiating to an acceptable offer keeps you in control of the outcome of your claim rather than having it decided by a judge.

You should view your claim as a business deal. You have suffered injury or incurred financial losses, and you expect to be compensated. You should not allow your natural bitterness towards the driver who has caused your problems to be a factor in negotiating a settlement, because this will cloud your judgment. You should not press for your 'day in court' just to make a point. Your legal advisors, the other driver's insurer and the judge will all deal with the matter objectively, and you should try to do so too.

Reaching an acceptable out-of-court settlement often means making concessions. You are unlikely to get back the cost of every expense which you think was caused by the accident. Few people limit their losses to the extent that the law requires. Many consider that they are entitled to hire a car or use taxis for a longer period than a judge may allow. Claims for expenses such as eating out, hotel accommodation and hiring a chauffeur will be allowed only in exceptional circumstances. Judges disapprove of what might be considered inflated claims, they call it 'over-egging the pudding' and it can serve to discredit the proper and reasonable items in your claim. Being flexible in negotiations on your expenses can often be fully compensated by achieving a better settlement offer for your injury.

If you accept an offer in full settlement of your claim, it is final and you cannot ask for more money at a later date. The exception to this is where provisional damages are awarded at trial. The medical evidence may indicate that there is more than a remote risk of you developing some other condition as a result of your injury. In those circumstances, it would be advisable to reject any offer of settlement which is to be final.

At the trial, the judge can be asked to make an award of provisional damages. The formal written details of your claim will have to be amended to include this. If your request is granted, you will be awarded damages on the basis of your known condition, but you will be able to return to court for a further assessment of damages if the identified different condition occurs in the future. An example of a possible future condition which is likely to attract provisional damages is epilepsy following a head injury.

## Interim payments

It might be the case that liability is not disputed but the claim cannot be settled yet. This will be because not all of the evidence has been obtained. You might be waiting to see how your injury progresses, or to have specialist treatment, before getting a final medical report.

If money worries are adding to your difficulties, it may be possible to get a sum in advance of settlement. This is called an interim payment. Your solicitor can ask the other side to make such a payment as settlement for particular items which are agreed, such as car repairs. An interim payment can also be made against your claim generally. The advantage to you is an easing of your financial difficulties. The advantage to the other driver's insurer is a reduction in the sum on which you can claim interest.

Your opponent might not agree to make an interim payment. Once a summons or writ has been issued, your solicitor can ask the court to make an order that you be paid an interim payment. The judge will consider a number of factors such as the total value of your claim, how much of it is agreed by the other side, and when the case might be ready for trial. He can refuse to make the order. If he does make an order, it may be for less than you have asked. You have no right to an interim payment and cannot demand one. However, a successful request for an interim payment will provide some relief while you are waiting for your claim to reach its conclusion.

If the other driver was not insured, you cannot get an interim payment. This is because an interim payment can only be ordered against a defendant who is backed by substantial funds or an insurer. The MIB will not make an interim payment, and none can be ordered against it. The MIB is only required to pay such sum as you are awarded by the court in a final judgment, although it will often make an offer to settle your claim without a judgment.

## Issuing proceedings

If negotiations break down, and in any case within three years of your accident if you suffered an injury, proceedings will be issued in court.

For high value claims, at least £50,000, your solicitor might issue in the High Court by means of a writ (strictly called a writ of summons). For most road accidents, a summons is issued in the county court. Apart from the difference in technical procedure, there might be tactical advantages in issuing in the High Court, which your solicitor will discuss with you if it is appropriate to your circumstances. Negotiations can continue with a view to settling your claim, but your solicitor will also begin to prepare your case for trial.

When proceedings have been issued, you will be called the plaintiff, an old form of the term complainant which is used in the USA. In Scotland you will be called the pursuer. The other driver is called the defendant (in Scotland, defender). The summons and details of your claim must be delivered to the defendant. Some defendants disappear, and it can be very difficult to achieve an effective service of the summons. It is the defendant you are claiming against, not his insurer. His insurer is only obliged to pay any award which you get at trial.

# 18 TAKING YOUR CLAIM TO TRIAL

If your opponent makes no acceptable offer to settle your claim, the matter will have to be decided by a judge at trial.

For claims of a value below £5,000, the trial will be by a District Judge, often in a room, the judge's chambers, rather than a formal courtroom, and he does not wear formal court dress. Claims of £5,000 and more will be in open court before a Circuit Judge, and actions in the High Court will be before a High Court Judge. The judge sits alone. There are no juries in road accident trials, the judge decides all matters of fact and law.

If liability for the accident is disputed, this will be considered first. It might be possible to agree the value of the various items of your claim, so that the trial is concerned only with the issue of liability to pay those damages. If liability for the accident has been admitted, the trial will be concerned only with whether the accident caused the losses claimed, and their value.

It is not important where the proceedings are issued, and your solicitor might issue in a court local to him. If it is necessary to attend court, the action can be transferred to a court which is convenient for most of the parties and witnesses.

## Witnesses

All evidence must be given in person unless that evidence is agreed by both sides or spoken evidence is not possible. The evidence of all witnesses must be disclosed to the other side once proceedings have been issued. You are also a witness, as you will give evidence of what happened and how it has affected you. Your solicitor will take a statement from you for this purpose.

All witnesses will be asked to give a list of dates when they would not be available to attend the trial. This information will help the court clerks to list the trial for the most convenient date, but they must take other considerations into account, and the trial date might be inconvenient to some of the participants. The fewer 'unavailable' dates notified to the court, the earlier the trial is likely to be.

If a witness is reluctant to attend the trial, your solicitor will issue a witness summons. This is an instruction to the witness by the court that he must attend the trial. If a witness ignores a witness summons, he is liable for financial penalties. In the High Court, a witness summons is called a subpoena (pronounced su-peena, meaning 'under a penalty').

## The trial

When an application has been made to the court office for a trial date, it might be listed in the 'warned' list. This means that it could be called-on at any time within the warned period, often at only twenty-four hours notice. The reason for the warned list is that many listed cases settle before trial, or take up less of the court's time than was expected. This means that other cases must be called forward to take the court time which has become free. Because of the uncertainty about whether listed cases will actually come to trial, the court listing clerks need to overbook the court. If there is less than the expected number of settlements or of trials ending sooner than expected, you may find that your case is not called on for the day which has been notified. You may be given a trial date but find your case in the 'floaters' list. Your case will then be called on as soon as a court, and judge, is available to hear your case.

At the trial your case will be presented by either your own solicitor, another solicitor from his firm, or a barrister. A person addressing the court is called an advocate. You may present your own case, or you can ask the judge if he will allow you to have someone, who is not a solicitor or barrister, to speak for you. The judge will want to be satisfied that the person you want to speak for you understands the rules of evidence and court procedure.

After outlining the case to the judge, your advocate will call you and other witnesses to give evidence. He will ask you questions designed to get the facts of your case before the court. This is called the examination in chief. The judge may order that the witness statements are to be the evidence of their makers, and you may be asked to read your statement to the court instead of your advocate asking you the questions of an examination in chief. After this, your opponent's advocate will be able to ask you questions, and this is called cross-examination. Your advocate will have an opportunity, called a re-examination, to ask you questions on any points raised in the cross-examination with a view to correcting any misleading impressions. The other side will then call their witnesses. There could be many witnesses, such as witnesses who saw the accident, agents who compiled the reports of the accident site, motor vehicle engineers, medical experts, accountants who compiled loss of earnings reports, employment consultants, or it may be the case that there is no one giving evidence except you. Your solicitor will have tried to get the evidence agreed by the other side to avoid having to call witnesses to prove every piece of evidence.

The judge might ask you some questions himself. There may then be some technical discussions between the lawyers and the judge about reported cases which either support you or go against you. Each advocate will make a concluding statement about their client's case. The judge will then run through the main points and say which version of events about the accident or its consequences he prefers, based on the evidence presented to him. He will decide who was to blame for the accident and then assess how much is to be awarded to you, if you are successful, under each head of claim.

Sometimes the judge cannot decide what his judgment should be on the day of the trial. He will read his notes of the evidence at a later time, and the court will send a written note of his judgment and the reasons for it to your solicitor. This is known as a reserved judgment. If there is not enough time to hear all the evidence or for the judge to give a detailed judgment, the trial will be continued on another day when that judge is available to hear the rest of the evidence and to deliver his judgment. This is called an adjournment part-heard.

When there is a strong dispute about who is to blame for the accident, it may be advisable to have the liability issue decided early. This ensures that the considerable expense of proving losses such as the cost of medical reports is not wasted if your claim fails on liability at a full trial. When there is a preliminary trial on liability it is called a split trial, the full trial on both liability and quantum being split into two trials. If you are successful with your split trial on liability, you can then concentrate on getting together the evidence for a trial concerned only with your provable losses and their value. Although it will be called an assessment of damages hearing, it is still a trial.

If your claim is worth less than £1,000 for injury, £3,000 if no injury, it will be automatically transferred to the small claims procedure of the County Court, which is also known as arbitration. In Scotland it is called summary cause. This is likely to be less formal in the way evidence is given. It is a procedure meant for people to use without being represented by a lawyer. However, if you are against an insurer, they will almost always instruct solicitors. You can instruct a solicitor to present your case, but you will not get back the cost of doing so as explained in chapter 15.

## Appeals

If you are dissatisfied with a judgment because you think that the court has made an error in law or has valued your claim too low, you can enter an appeal. An appeal from the judgment of a District Judge is to a Circuit Judge and must be filed within fourteen days. An appeal from a Circuit Judge is to the Court of Appeal. Notice of an intention to appeal must be given within four weeks. If you wish to appeal to the House of Lords from the decision of the Court of Appeal, you will have to have been given leave by one of those courts. The House of Lords will usually only hear appeals which involve important points of law. Appeals in Scotland are from the Sheriff court to the Court of Session, and from there to the House of Lords in London.

# 19 YOUR SETTLEMENT

The total sum you receive as compensation is called a settlement if it is agreed, or an award if it is decided by the judge at trial. It includes any interim payments, and also the money you have received in state benefits which are deducted and repaid to the DSS. For simplicity, I will refer to your compensation as a settlement.

A substantial settlement is intended to compensate for future losses and expenses, but it can easily be spent in a fairly short time. Careful thought should be given to how the settlement is to be dealt with. If you receive a large lump sum, you should seek early advice on prudent investment so that you are not facing a completely bleak financial future in the years after the settlement is received.

Your solicitor may be able to suggest a suitable financial adviser. You should consider making a Will, or reviewing the provisions of an existing Will, as the value of your estate will have now increased.

In appropriate cases, a structured settlement may be agreed. Instead of paying a lump sum, your opponent's insurance company buys an annuity for you. This is a type of pension, so that you receive an annual sum for life, so ensuring that the money will never run out completely. This arrangement has tax advantages to you, and it can be linked to the retail prices index so that its value is not eroded by inflation. It is usually possible to take some money as a lump sum for immediate capital expenses. This might be for alterations to your house to accommodate, for instance, a wheelchair. The bulk of the money would go into the structured settlement.

You may need to consider the effect of your settlement on any state benefits you are receiving. You might have been receiving one or more of these, such as income support, before the accident. Your settlement will give you a capital sum which may be more than the maximum you can have to still qualify for the benefits. Your settlement may mean that you will no longer get the benefits. Loss of income support leads to loss of housing benefit, council tax benefit and exemption from prescription charges. The effect is to seriously reduce the value to you of your compensation.

This loss can be overcome by setting up a trust for your settlement. The money is held on trust by a trustee, so the money is not your capital. The trustee can give you sums out of the trust fund to pay certain expenses such as a holiday or house extension, but not for living expenses, without affecting your benefits. A properly constituted trust will not be treated as if you had deprived yourself of capital in order to obtain state benefits. This is a complex area of law, and you will have to spend some of your compensation on legal fees to get expert advice.

## Solicitor's costs

If you have funded the claim yourself, you will have a contract with your solicitor to pay his fees and expenses regardless of the outcome of your claim. If your claim is successful, your solicitor will try to recover as much of your costs from the other side as he can. This has been discussed in chapter 15. It is likely that there will be a shortfall between the amount of costs which your solicitor can recover for you and what you must pay to him. Your compensation will therefore be reduced by some legal costs.

## The Legal Aid statutory charge

If you have Legal Aid, the comments made under

'solicitors costs' above will also apply. The Legal Aid Board is required to keep its outlay to a minimum. It must therefore recover its payments to your solicitor for his fees and expenses if at all possible. The reimbursement of the board's outlay will come first from the other side and any shortfall from you. When you are granted Legal Aid, a statutory charge, a charge required by the Legal Aid Act, attaches to any money you recover in your claim. You must therefore repay to the Legal Aid Board the costs which have not been recovered from the other side.

## Contractual sick pay

You may have been paid by your employer while you were off work because of the accident. You may have a contractual obligation to repay this from your compensation. Your employer will provide you with a copy of the contract terms and a calculation of the sum to be repaid. You will need these documents to prove this head of claim, which will be added to your schedule of Special Damages. It is a form of loan from your employer which you only have to repay if you are successful in getting compensation.

Contractual sick pay is not really a deduction, because it is first added to your claim to take account of the requirement to repay it to your employer. However, when you receive a settlement sum, you will need to remember that it includes contractual sick pay which must be deducted. You are responsible for repaying the contractual sick pay to your employer.

## State Benefits

If you are unable to work because of your injury, you might receive state benefits such as incapacity benefit. The DSS will recover these benefits from your compensation if it is more than £2,500. This is fair if you recover your loss of earnings, because otherwise the state benefits would be an overpayment. You will have received more for being off work than you would have received had you remained at work.

The other driver's insurer will register details of your claim with the Compensation Recovery Unit of the DSS. The CRU will issue a certificate detailing the benefits paid to you as a result of the accident and which they can recover. The insurer will deduct this sum from the compensation to be paid to you, and pay it over to the CRU.

Compensation for property damage is not taken into account. For example: Your car repairs cost £1000 and compensation for injury and loss of earnings is £2000, total compensation £3000. You have received £3000 in state benefits. Only £2000 of state benefits would be deducted because the sum received by you for car repairs, being property damage, is not taken into account. (Please note at end of chapter.)

If you were unemployed at the date of the accident, you will have no claim for loss of earnings. Your unemployment benefit (soon to change to jobseeker's allowance) will stop because you will no longer be available for work because of your injury, and you will be paid incapacity benefit instead. This benefit will be deducted from your compensation for pain, suffering and loss of amenity. It was originally thought that this injustice was a result of the Government rushing to put this law into effect and not giving proper thought to all of its effects. However, the unfair effect of this rule was brought to the notice of the Government, but nothing was done to correct it. It was not uncommon for an unemployed person to have all of his compensation for his injury taken by the CRU, even though the DSS had paid to him little more, if any, than was being paid to him in unemployment benefit before the accident. The Court of Appeal has recently confirmed that the recoupment of benefits regulations allow deductions to be made from the compensation for pain and suffering. The court suggested that a claim could be made for lost unemployment benefit. This overturns the previous argument that, although a claimant ceases to be entitled to unemployment benefit if he is not fit enough to look for work, he loses nothing because unemployment benefit is replaced by incapacity benefit.

Other state benefits which will be deducted, if paid as a consequence of the accident, include attendance allowance, income support, family credit, reduced earnings allowance, severe disablement allowance, disability living allowance and disability working allowance.

If your settlement is not more than £2,500, the CRU will not require a refund of benefits. However, the compensator is entitled to deduct a sum equal to half of the benefits you have received. This is a windfall for the defendant and his insurer. In practice, insurers do not usually take advantage of this right.

## Contributory negligence

### *Liability*

You may be held to have contributed to the cause of the accident. Your award at court or an agreed settlement figure will be reduced in proportion to your liability. If liability is 50:50, you will receive half of the value of your claim. If liability is 75:25 in your favour, you will receive three-quarters (75%) of the value of your claim.

Even a passenger can be held to have contributed to the fact that he has suffered a loss. You should not travel with a driver you suspect has been drinking. If you do, and an accident occurs which is the driver's fault, there could be a reduction in your compensation because you knowingly accepted the risk of an accident.

### *Quantum*

Even though you are blameless concerning the cause of the accident, you may have contributed to your own injury or other losses. If you were not wearing your seatbelt or, as a cyclist or motorcyclist, not wearing a helmet, your injury might be more serious than if you had taken proper measures to protect yourself. In this case, there will be a deduction from your compensation to take account of the contribution you have made to your injury.

## Tax

Your compensation is not taxable during your lifetime. Income such as interest or dividends on invested compensation is taxable as unearned income in the normal way. On your death, any remaining compensation forms part of your estate and may be subject to inheritance tax if the net value of your estate, that is, after payment of debts, exceeds the tax threshold.

## Your spouse's share

Your settlement becomes your capital. Your spouse will have a claim on it in the event of divorce in the same way that such a claim attaches to other assets, except for any sum specifically required for your future care. The fact that money was awarded to you for past and future pain and suffering does not protect it from being included in the pot for distribution on divorce. It has happened, sadly not infrequently, that a spouse has felt unable to remain with a badly injured partner. The accident victim loses both a spouse and much of the money compensation. It may be worth discussing with your solicitor any possible trust arrangements which might protect you from this, but it is unlikely that your compensation can be fully insulated from the demands of a divorce settlement.

## Your creditors' share

If you become bankrupt, a trustee in bankruptcy will be appointed to deal with your financial affairs. His job is to try to pay something from your assets and income to your creditors. Any compensation you receive will go into the pool of assets for distribution. The trustee can take full control of your claim, as your expectation of compensation is itself an asset which is saleable. Your legal right to bring a claim can be assigned to someone else. The trustee is more likely to run the claim to a negotiated settlement or award at trial. As with your other financial affairs as a bankrupt, your wishes will have little influence in the matter.

## Additions

If your claim goes to trial, your lawyer can ask the judge to award you interest on the sum you receive in compensation. The interest rates are different for special damages and general damages and are fixed by court rules.

NOTE
The government is under renewed pressure to exempt compensation for pain and suffering from the state benefits recoupment provisions. The House of Commons Social Security Committee has recommended that benefits should be recouped only from compensation for special damages, and not from general damages. However, this still means that the deduction can be made from reimbursement for expenses incurred because of the accident.

The committee has also recommended that the recoupment should take account of any reduction in compensation because of contributory negligence. This would mean that the amount of recoupable benefits would be reduced by the same proportion as the reduction in compensation.

# 20 GETTING YOUR MONEY

## A pre-trial settlement

If you have agreed an out-of-court settlement with your opponent's insurer, you will usually not have to wait long for the money. If there has not been a payment into court, your settlement cheque will be requested from that insurer. The settlement is a binding agreement, and your solicitor will need your written approval of the settlement before he will accept it on your behalf. The agreement should specify a maximum time for the cheque to reach your solicitor, twenty-eight days being reasonable. It should also make provision for the payment of your legal costs. If the cheque does not arrive within the agreed time, you can consider yourself no longer bound by the settlement agreement and proceed to trial.

If proceedings have been issued, the settlement terms will be set out in a consent order which will be sent to the court for approval. Except where the plaintiff is a minor or under a mental disability, court approval will be granted without the need for anyone to attend. The consent order, when sealed by the court (it is now an ink stamp), becomes a judgment of the court. Your opponent can only pay money into court as a settlement offer if proceedings have been issued. Acceptance of the sum paid into court in full and final satisfaction of your claim, within twenty-one days of it being paid in, is done by filing a notice of acceptance at court and serving a copy on your opponent. You will be entitled to your legal costs as well. If the agreed settlement is more than the money in court, with the payer agreeing to send a cheque for the additional sum, a consent order is needed. If the sum in court is accepted within the time allowed, the court will send it to your solicitor quite quickly. After twenty-one days, the court will pay the money into the court central funds account in London. Payment out of this central account takes longer, but not usually more than six weeks.

## A court judgment

If your case is decided at trial, your solicitor will receive a written judgment stating the sum which has been awarded to you. If an insurer or the MIB are involved on behalf of your opponent, they will usually pay reasonably promptly, within about four weeks, once they receive a copy of the judgment, unless they intend to appeal the decision. If the money, or some of it, has been paid into court, it will be paid out by the court funds office. It is not advisable to spend money, or commit yourself to a large expense, in anticipation of receiving your settlement cheque. It can be delayed for any number of reasons.

## The private payer

If a defendant does not have an insurer or the MIB to pay the judgment, and he does not volunteer to pay it or make satisfactory instalment proposals, you will have to enforce the judgment. There are a number of ways of enforcing a judgment, and you will have to choose carefully which ones are most likely to be successful in your case. If one method fails, you can try another one, but you will be incurring costs at each stage. You have six years to enforce your judgment. If you are prepared to wait for the defendant, now called the judgment debtor, to come into money, you must apply to court to extend this period before the six years have expired. It is possible to resurrect an expired judgment debt, but a court order is needed, and you will have to persuade the judge that there was a good reason for letting the time expire. If, before the six years expire, the judgment debtor acknowledges the debt, a fresh six year enforcement period begins.

You can find out details of a debtor's means by having him orally examined by an officer of the court. You can put questions to the debtor about his income, assets and other debts. The debtor's replies to the questions are put into an affidavit which can be used against him if he has lied. If a debtor refuses to attend for an oral examination, he can be sent to prison for contempt of court.

## Warrant of execution

This is an order for the court bailiff to take the goods of the judgment debtor and to sell them at auction. After the sale, if sufficient money is obtained after the costs of sale have been deducted, you will receive all or part of your judgment sum and costs, including the warrant fee. Any balance will be paid over to the debtor. This procedure is called levying distress. It is often not very successful as it is rather easy to resist. The High Court sheriff is generally more successful. If you have a High Court judgment, or your county court judgment is for more than £2,000 and you transfer it to the High Court, you can get the sheriff's officer to seize the debtor's goods by issuing a writ of *fieri facias* (usually abbreviated to *fi fa*, pronounced like high-hay, see the glossary of legal terms).

## Attachment of earnings

If the debtor is in regular employment, you can apply to court for an attachment of earnings order against him. This will direct the debtor's employer to deduct sums from his earnings and pay them into court. The order will usually only be made after a hearing, at which the judge will consider what the debtor can reasonably afford to pay. If the debtor leaves his job, you can have the order redirected to his new employer. The debtor is required to inform the court of any change of employment.

## Garnishee order

If you know of someone who owes money to the judgment debtor, you can apply for an order that they pay the money owed into court instead. This order is most often directed to the debtor's bank. There are often difficulties in getting details of the debtor's account number. You will also need to get the order served at the right time, being when there is more than a nominal sum credited to his account. The details of debts owed to the debtor, which you will need for your request for a garnishee order, might be obtained from an oral examination of him.

## Charging order

If the court will grant you a charging order, you can have this registered against the debtor's house. The debt becomes a type of mortgage on the house. When the debtor comes to sell it, he will have to pay his debt to you so that you remove the charge, because no-one will buy a house with a charge registered against it. If the judgment debt is substantial, you can apply to court for an order for sale. The house will be sold by order of the court, and the proceeds will be applied to satisfy the debts secured by registered charges in order of priority. If the debtor bought the house with a mortgage loan, this will already be registered and will be paid off first. Your debt will be paid out of any surplus after all debts secured by prior registered charges are satisfied.

## Bankruptcy

If your judgment debt is more than £750, you can

petition the court for the debtor to be declared bankrupt. This may not assist you except to the extent that the threat of it may persuade the debtor to pay you something to avoid bankruptcy. A judgment debt is like any other debt in this regard. You will need to serve the debtor with a properly completed form called a Statutory Demand. It sets out details of the debt and requires that payment be made within twenty-one days.

A failure to satisfy a statutory demand is accepted as proof of the debtor's insolvency, and a bankruptcy petition can then be presented to the court. Alternatively, a warrant of execution which has been returned to you by the court bailiff or sheriff, because seizure of goods was unsuccessful, is also proof of insolvency. A hearing will be arranged for the debtor to oppose the petition. If the debtor is declared bankrupt, the court appoints a person to be the trustee in bankruptcy. He will deal with any assets the debtor has, and will try to settle any debts that have been notified to him. There may be creditors who have a priority in the queue to be paid. These are called preferential creditors, and might include the Inland Revenue for unpaid tax, Customs and Excise for unpaid VAT, and a bank or building society in respect of the mortgage on the debtor's house.

## Registration of judgments

Your unsatisfied judgment will automatically be registered in the Register of county court judgments after one month. This will not get you any money, and will only serve to make it difficult for the debtor to get credit. However, if you have no other remedy against the debtor, this might give you at least some small measure of comfort. There is no equivalent registration scheme for High Court judgments.

## Interest

You are entitled to add interest to your unsatisfied judgment debt from the date of judgment at the prescribed annual rate, currently 8%. If you have a county court judgment, the debt must be at least £5,000 for interest to be added.

# 21 TIME FACTORS

Pursuing a road accident claim always takes much longer than you expect. There are many reasons for this, and some of them are discussed here:

## Evidence

Your opponent will not pay your claim unless you prove your losses. You must establish that it is more probable than not that you have suffered the losses you claim. Your solicitor might need to get a motor vehicle assessor's report on your car, details of your pay from your employer, a photographic report of the accident site, witness statements, and a medical report of your injury.

If you have not recovered from your injury, you cannot know what effect it will have on your life in the future. It is therefore not possible to estimate a value for your claim at that time. Your solicitor will advise you to delay settling your claim until it is clearer what the future effects of your injury might be. He might recommend that you delay trying to settle your claim in order to obtain a further medical report after a period of six months or a year. You would then have a clearer prognosis, an idea of what to expect from your injury in the future. Once you have accepted a settlement of your injury claim, you cannot usually go back to the other driver or his insurer later to ask for more money because your injury is worse than you had thought.

It might become evident only after many months that you cannot return to your job, or that you cannot do your job properly, because of your injury. You might not have noticed how much heavy lifting you have to do in your job until you have suffered an injury.

The assessment of your loss of earnings might have to be done by accountants, and an employment consultant might be needed to assess your future employment prospects. Your solicitor might have to ask you to obtain quotations for the cost of help with housework, for gardening and for periodic decorating of your home if you can no longer do these things yourself.

## Rules of court

Your opponent is entitled to take advantage of the rules of court to oppose your claim or to require full evidence in support of it. He can oppose your solicitor's attempts to bring the matter to an early trial. He can require you to give replies to a list of questions, called interrogatories, and he can ask the court for more time to investigate your claim. Your opponent can, and often will, require you to be examined by his own medical expert. This adds to the delay. All medical experts are much in demand for legal reports and an appointment can often be six or nine months away.

## Time limits

You must issue legal proceedings within the time allowed by law. This is usually three years for claims involving injury and six years for most other claims. Accidents involving travel on ships and aircraft may be subject to a two-year limit, and there is even a one-year limitation in some circumstances involving fare-paying travel by road. Except in ships and aircraft cases, the time runs from when you ought to know that you have grounds for a claim and who the defendant ought to be. If you are knocked unconscious in the accident, the time will not begin to run until you recover consciousness and are aware that you have suffered an injury. Time does not begin to run for children until they reach eighteen.

Failure to issue proceedings in time is a defence to the action. The court can allow an action to proceed even if it was issued out of time, but there must be persuasive reasons for it to do so. If you think you are out of time for making a claim, consider getting preliminary legal advice on your chances of beating the time bar.

The summons or writ must be delivered to the defendant within four months of issue. If the defendant has disappeared, an application to court can be made to extend this time. If necessary, an application can be made for leave to serve the summons on someone else such as the defendant's insurance company.

The defendant must send a defence to your action to the court within fourteen days of the service of the summons, unless an extension of time is agreed. If no defence is entered, you can apply for a judgment that you are entitled to compensation for the losses which you can prove. An assessment of damages hearing will then be arranged. The defendant can apply to have your judgment set aside, and he is likely to succeed if he can show that it is reasonable to contest your claim.

In the county court, if the defendant does not file a defence at court, or if he files an admission that your claim has merit, you must apply to court for judgment on liability within twelve months or your claim will be struck out. You must apply to court to have your case set down in the list for trial within six months of a defence being entered. If no application for a trial is made within fifteen months of the filing of the defence, your action will be struck out. The court can be asked to extend these time limits.

# 22 SOME THINGS THAT CAN GO WRONG WITH YOUR CLAIM

1 You are injured as a passenger and you knew or suspected that your driver, who was to blame, is not insured. You can only look to him to pay your damages, and he might not have the means. The MIB will not assist you.

2 Your car is damaged but you are not injured. The other driver did not stop, or he gave you a false name and address. There is no one to claim against. The MIB untraced driver scheme is for claims for injury or death only.

3 You do not issue a summons in time, within three years from the accident if you are claiming for injury. The defendant has a statutory defence.

4 You have a name and address for the other driver and the summons is sent off. It is returned marked 'Gone Away', and the four months period allowed for serving the summons has expired. Your claim cannot proceed because you have failed to serve the summons in time.

5 You have served the summons, but a defence to it has not been filed at court. You do not apply for judgment for twelve months because you are gathering evidence to prove your losses. Your claim is struck out.

6 You have served the summons, and the defendant files an admission of liability to pay for such losses as you prove. You continue to collect evidence and

to negotiate towards a possible settlement, but you do not apply for an interlocutory judgment within twelve months. Your claim is struck out.

7 You do not apply for a trial date within fifteen months of receiving a defence. Your claim is struck out.

8 The defendant lies at the trial, and the judge believes him. He may get other people to say that they saw the accident and that the defendant was not at fault, even though you know that they were never there. If the other driver and his witnesses are credible at trial, your claim is likely to fail.

9 You are injured by a cyclist, or his bicycle damages your car. The cyclist is not required by law to have insurance and, in your case, he is not insured. His liability to compensate you is not covered by the MIB scheme. If he does not have personal liability insurance under his household insurance, and he does not have the means to pay, you will not get any compensation. Your own comprehensive insurance would take care of damage to your car, but you will lose your no claims discount.

10 You sustain injury in your accident, but you press your solicitor to settle your claim early. However, you do not recover as quickly as you thought you would. Also, your employer now wants you to do work which is more physically demanding. This is difficult because of the continuing discomfort of your injury, and your job is at risk. Your claim is now clearly worth more than you settled for, but the matter is closed.

# 23 DEFENDING A CLAIM

If you are a driver involved in an accident and you think that you were at fault, do not make any admissions, or even express any regret for what happened, to anyone. Apart from giving details of your name, address and insurer, it is advisable to say nothing at all. You may feel callous, and you might well be criticized, but any form of admission might invalidate the indemnity provided by your insurance. If your insurance company is able to invalidate the policy, it could settle the other driver's claim, and the claims of any passengers, and then claim the money back from you. Report the details of the accident to your insurer as soon as possible. If you receive a summons send it to your insurer immediately. Time is very short. If a defence is not filed within fourteen days, judgment could be entered against you without you having a chance to put your side of the case.

If you were insured, your insurer will deal with matters and instruct solicitors where appropriate if you have a viable defence. You will be required to assist them with a statement and possibly attending trial. If you were not insured, the MIB will ask you to agree to them dealing with the claim and that you will reimburse their outlay. This is likely to be the cheapest option, as the MIB will defend the claim if possible, or negotiate a settlement, and the legal costs will be much less than if the matter goes to trial.

If you were not insured and you want to dispute the claim yourself, you must file a defence in time and it must dispute each allegation in the particulars of claim. Anything which is not specifically denied is presumed to be admitted. A simple denial of liability will not do.

## Defences

Apart from the facts of the accident and any witnesses who are in your favour, there may be other defences to the claim against you.

1 The plaintiff has waited too long to issue proceedings against you. This is three years from the accident if the claim includes injury, otherwise it is six years.

2 You do not owe a duty of care to the plaintiff. In *Pitts* v. *Hunt,* which is mentioned in chapter 1, the passenger encouraged the driver to drive dangerously. There is also *Ashton* v. *Turner* (1981) where the plaintiff and the defendant had been together on a burglary, and the defendant crashed the getaway car. Both had been drinking heavily before the incident. The court said that, on the grounds of public policy, there was no duty of care between participants in crime.

3 The plaintiff passenger consented to the risk. He knew that you were intoxicated, or for some other reason likely to drive badly or dangerously, when he agreed to travel with you.

4 The plaintiff becomes bankrupt after the accident. He cannot continue with his action because he cannot pay your costs if he loses the case. However, his trustee in bankruptcy can elect to continue the claim if security for costs is given.

## Counter-claim

Even if you think that the other driver was entirely at fault, he might be the first to issue legal proceedings. You will then be the defendant in the action. As well as defending the other driver's claim, and the claims of any of his passengers, you can also claim against him in the same proceedings. This is called a counter-claim. If the case is not settled by negotiation but goes to trial, the other driver's claim will be dealt with first. If he succeeds completely on liability so that you are held fully to blame, your counter-claim will not be considered. If the judge decides that the other driver was wholly or partly to blame, your counter-claim will be considered. An award will be made on the evidence of your counter-claim, and then be reduced by the proportion that blame for the accident attaches to you, if any. There might be a further reduction to take account of any contribution by you to the extent of your losses, such as failing to wear a seat belt.

## Third party notice

If the other driver did not own the car he was driving, and he suffered no loss to himself in the accident, the car's owner might sue you for the damage to his car and loss of its use. If you think that the other driver was at fault, you should join him to the action by issuing a third party notice. This will tell all parties concerned, and the court, that you say that the other driver caused all or some of the losses which the car owner is claiming. Where two or more persons are in a legal relationship, whether it is concerning a contract or legal proceedings, any other person who is not in that relationship is called a third party. You can also include your own claim against the other driver in your third party notice. You cannot counter-claim against the car owner because he has not caused your losses. Where a third party notice has been issued in these circumstances, the car owner should consider amending his summons to include the driver of his car as a defendant. If he does not do that, he will get less, or nothing at all, if the driver of his car is held partly or fully liable for the accident.

## Contribution Notice

If you are one of two or more defendants in the action, you should consider serving a contribution notice on the other defendants. This is because two or more defendants, called joint defendants, might be held jointly and severally liable to compensate the plaintiff. Severally means that the plaintiff can look to any one of the defendants to pay his compensation. A contribution notice informs the other defendants that you will look to them to pay all or some of any judgment made against you. A common occurrence is a multiple rear-end shunt. A queue of traffic is stationary. A vehicle approaching the queue fails to stop and hits the end car of the queue, pushing it into the car in front. There is a domino effect, with cars being pushed from behind into the car in front. A car owner or driver should sue all of the drivers behind him if none of them admits full responsibility for the accident. Those drivers should then serve contribution notices on the drivers who were behind them.

Your insurer may settle your opponent's claim, even though you think that you were not to blame and that the claim should be defended. Your insurer takes a commercial view, and may decide that settling the claim will be cheaper than defending it. This does not prevent you from proceeding with a counter-claim. Your opponent will be encouraged by what he might see as your insurer conceding defeat, but it will not affect your counter-claim if the settlement was made with no admission of liability.

If your insurer goes out of business after an accident which results in a claim against you, the Policyholders' Protection Board should be asked to meet any judgment against you.

# 24 SUGGESTED DOs AND DON'Ts

## DO

1 **DO** keep a camera, notebook and pen in your car in case of need.

2 **DO** inform your own insurer about the accident.

3 **DO** report the accident to the Police and request a written report.

4 **DO** keep a diary of the events following the accident until your claim is settled.

5 **DO** respond to letters promptly. Write legibly on A4 paper with a wide left-hand margin to assist with filing. Include your solicitor's reference, and date the letter. The date is the means of identifying it from your other letters.

6 **DO** tell your solicitor of any relevant changes in your circumstances such as a change of address (this may seem obvious, but many don't), another accident or illness or change of job.

7 **DO** get receipts when incurring expenses caused by the accident.

8 **DO** be realistic about what can be achieved by your claim. Your solicitor will advise you about this.

9 **DO** take reasonable steps to try to limit your losses.

10 **DO** be very careful of what you write or say to anyone about the other driver or anybody else. You could give them grounds to bring an action in libel or slander if you cannot prove that what you say is true.

## DON'T

1 **DON'T** be determined to teach the other driver a lesson, and to get a judgment against him at all costs.

2 **DON'T** refuse to pay for expenses such as car repairs, waiting for the other driver to pay because the accident was his fault, not yours. The court will not be sympathetic to your view.

3 **DON'T** take notice of anything you read or hear about other claims. The circumstances of your own claim will be very different.

4 **DON'T** leave work voluntarily, instead be dismissed on medical grounds.

5 **DON'T** ignore minor injuries. Visit your doctor so that the injuries are recorded in your medical notes. Failing to visit your doctor shortly after the accident might be used by your opponent to challenge your claim that your injury was caused by the accident.

6 **DON'T** exaggerate your injury or other losses. Your opponent is likely to detect it, and it may prejudice the genuine parts of your claim. Also, don't be tempted to lie in court. It would be perjury, which is a serious criminal offence.

7 **DON'T** be intimidated by the legal process. Your solicitor will help you to understand it, and to cope with attending a trial if it becomes necessary.

8 **DON'T** expect your claim to be a simple six months affair, as it can often be long and tedious.

9 **DON'T** expect the Judge to accept what you say just because you know it to be true. You have to prove it.

10\. **DON'T** give up. Persevere as long as your solicitor advises that you have a fair prospect of success.

# 25 HOW TO COMPLAIN

## Your solicitor

If you are not satisfied with the progress of your claim, you should ask your solicitor about it. Be sure to be specific about the cause of your dissatisfaction. Your solicitor might not seem very sympathetic about your problems. This is because he must remain objective and advise you on what view of your claim a judge, who will be objective, is likely to take.

Your solicitor cannot get you compensation for losses which are not recognized at law. These might include interest on your borrowings, the fact that your car or house has been repossessed or the break-up of a relationship. It might seem unfair, but your solicitor has limitations on what he can do for you.

If you are not satisfied with your solicitor's response to your complaint, ask him to refer it to the person designated to deal with such complaints. All solicitors' firms are required to have a complaints-handling procedure. A different solicitor who holds a senior position at the firm will consider and respond to your complaint.

You are responsible for pursuing your claim correctly and within the timetable allowed. However, if you have instructed a solicitor to act for you and he misses a deadline so that your claim is struck out, or you suffer some other prejudice, you may have a remedy against him. You should consult a different firm of solicitors to advise you about this.

## The Solicitors Complaints Bureau

If you are not satisfied with the response of your solicitor and his firm to your complaint, you can send written details to the Solicitors Complaints Bureau. The bureau will expect you to have taken the matter up with the solicitor's firm initially and given them an opportunity to write to you with an explanation. Many frivolous complaints are made to the bureau. They are often the result of general frustration with the claim, which is often made worse by the discomfort of injuries and financial difficulties. Consideration is being given to the introduction of a modest application fee to filter out those complaints which are totally unreasonable. The equivalent professional body for dealing with complaints against barristers is the General Council of the Bar.

## The Legal Services Ombudsman

You might find yourself dissatisfied with how the professional body has dealt with your complaint. You can then refer it to the Legal Services Ombudsman. There is no charge. You can obtain an application form from the office of the Legal Services Ombudsman. You must complete and return this form within three months of being informed of the professional body's decision on your complaint. The ombudsman's officer will obtain the file of your case and make a report.

If the ombudsman is satisfied with the report, he will send a copy to you and to the professional body. The report might make criticisms or recommendations concerning how your complaint has been dealt with. The ombudsman can recommend that you be paid compensation if your complaint to him was justified. The lawyer of the professional body complained of must tell the ombudsman, within three months, what they have done in respect of his recommendations. If they do not, he can require them to make their reasons public. The Legal Services Ombudsman cannot investigate a matter which is the subject of a hearing at court or another tribunal.

## Court staff

If you are dissatisfied with the way your claim has been dealt with by the court staff, you can complain to the chief clerk of the court concerned. If you are not satisfied with his response, you can write with details to the Lord Chancellor's Department.

# 26 THE LEGAL SYSTEM

The purpose of this chapter is to give you a thumbnail sketch of the legal system, which exists to give you a remedy for harm caused to you. It is regrettable that most people learn about our legal system only when they find themselves involved with it. It would seem that the planners of our education system continue to believe that knowledge of algebra and the lives of medieval monarchs is more useful to us than is knowledge of our basic legal rights and obligations, and the means of enforcing them.

English law, which also applies in Wales, and is not very different in Northern Ireland, follows decisions which have been made in disputed cases in the past. This is called common law. Your right to compensation for harm done to you in a road accident is enforced by a common law action for another's negligence. The USA, Canada, Australia and many other countries which were once administered by Britain have a legal system which originated with English common law. In Scotland the legal system, like that of much of continental Europe, is derived from Roman law, although common law has an influence.

In addition to common law, many rules are made to control our conduct for the public good. This is called statute law, and must be approved by Parliament. The purpose of law is to achieve justice. Sometimes, however, these two concepts are in conflict. Justice demands that an offender must be to blame for his offence, but there are regulatory crimes which, for administrative convenience, are necessarily enforced against persons regardless of blame. If one of your car's rear lights fails, you immediately commit an offence, indeed a continuing offence all the while you are driving, although you are not aware of it. This is law but not justice.

Occasionally, a judge will bend the rules to achieve justice. If faced with an earlier case which goes against a deserving plaintiff, the judge might find some 'inconsistency' between the two cases so that he does not have to follow the earlier case. This is justice but not law. A simple example is where you fail at trial because your evidence is not strong enough to support you. The law requires that you prove your claim. You might not think that you have got justice in these circumstances.

## Criminal law

A crime is an offence against society. In the old terminology, but still true, it is an offence against the Queen's peace in her realm, meaning the peace and protection which she promises to her subjects. That is why the title of a criminal action is often *R* v. *Smith* (or whatever the accused's name is) meaning it is Regina (the Queen) against Smith. Criminal prosecutions are intended to be a civilized alternative to acts of revenge. The victim of a crime is not a party to the criminal action except as a witness. The prosecution of a criminal is intended to satisfy the victim, and also society generally, that appropriate measures have been taken against the criminal which might also act as a deterrent to others. The criminal law system is not meant to compensate individuals for their losses, although the courts do have a limited power to award compensation to victims of crime. Also, victims of violent crime can apply to the Criminal Injuries Compensation Board for an award for physical and mental injury suffered as a result of a criminal act.

Criminal offenders appear first in the Magistrates Court where the Magistrates must decide if they have the power to deal with the offence. Those offences not dealt with to a conclusion by the Magistrates will go to the Crown Court to be tried by a jury on matters of fact, with a judge presiding and deciding matters of law.

If a driver causes you injury and loss by the manner of his driving, he might not have committed a criminal offence. If he has committed an offence, such as inconsiderate driving, driving a defective vehicle or driving without insurance, this is quite distinct from your civil claim for compensation. If the other driver is convicted of a driving offence, as distinct from a documents offence such as no licence or insurance, this can be pleaded in support of your civil claim, although it is not conclusive. A driver might be convicted of speeding but, unless his excessive speed contributed to the accident, it is not relevant to your claim.

A motorist who has, in your view, clearly committed a driving offence, might be acquitted. This is because the standard of proof in criminal matters is much higher than in civil matters. It is necessary to prove, beyond a reasonable doubt, that the accused committed the offence. Even though the other driver may be acquitted of driving without due care, you can still allege careless driving by implication in your civil claim where the standard of proof is lower. The particulars of negligence set out in your particulars of claim are likely to imply careless driving by the defendant.

## Civil law

A civil claim is like a business deal. If you can prove, on a balance of probabilities, that the other driver caused your losses, the civil law will help you to obtain compensation for those losses. It is a private matter between you and him, and the state takes no interest in it other than to set the rules which must be followed if the assistance of the court has been requested. These rules, for instance, protect the interests of children who make a claim. Only rarely, as in family law matters, will the civil court become involved without the request of one of the parties to a dispute.

Most claims are issued in the county court and will be heard by a district judge or, where the value claimed exceeds £5000, a circuit judge. These are judges who travel round the various court centres on their circuit to hear appropriate cases. There is no longer an upper limit in value for claims which can be issued in the county court in England and Wales. There is a county court in most large towns.

In England, higher value claims, at least £25,000 unless a difficult point of law is involved, can be issued in the High Court. There is only one High Court, in the Strand in London and having over forty courtrooms. There are also branches of the High Court in many towns, usually in the same building as the county court, and these are called District Registries of the High Court. The High Court sits in three divisions dealing with different categories of case. These divisions are called Queen's Bench, Chancery and Family. Claims arising from a road accident will be issued in the Queen's Bench division. High Court judges travel out from London to hear cases at certain designated High Court trial centres in the provinces. These are county courts which double as High Court trial centres. Appeals from the county court and the High Court are to the Court of Appeal (civil division) and then, with leave, to the House of Lords.

In Scotland, the equivalent of the Magistrates court is the District court . The Sheriff court hears both criminal and civil cases. Appeal from the District court and the Sheriff court in criminal cases is to the High Court of Justiciary sitting as an appeals court. The most serious criminal cases begin in the High Court of Justiciary sitting as a court of first instance, with appeals being heard by that court sitting for appeals.

Civil cases can be issued in the Sheriff court or the Court of Session, which has a similar function to the English High Court. Cases begin in the Outer House of the Court of Session, while the Inner house is an appeal court. Appeals from the Sheriff court in civil cases can be to the Sheriff Principal, a high judicial and administration official with no equivalent in England, or to the Court of Session.

All of the jurisdictions in the British Isles have the adversarial system of trial. This means that the parties are adversaries, seeking to persuade the judge (or jury in criminal trials) to grant them what they ask by proving their case. This differs from the inquisitorial system of France and many other countries where the judge will investigate the claims of the parties and look for evidence.

## The Courts

The Magistrates court has some civil law functions such as licensing, statutory debt such as council tax, and some areas of family law. There is an appeal, in writing only, from the Magistrates court in criminal matters to the High Court. These functions are unlikely to be relevant to a road accident claim and are omitted from the following diagram for the sake of clarity.

## The English and Welsh courts

**Civil** | **Criminal**

Magistrates
↓
Crown Court → Court of Appeal (criminal division)

County Court → Court of Appeal (civil division)

High Court
(Queen's Bench/Chancery/family) → Court of Appeal (civil division)

Court of Appeal
civil division   criminal division
↓
House of Lords

## The Scottish courts

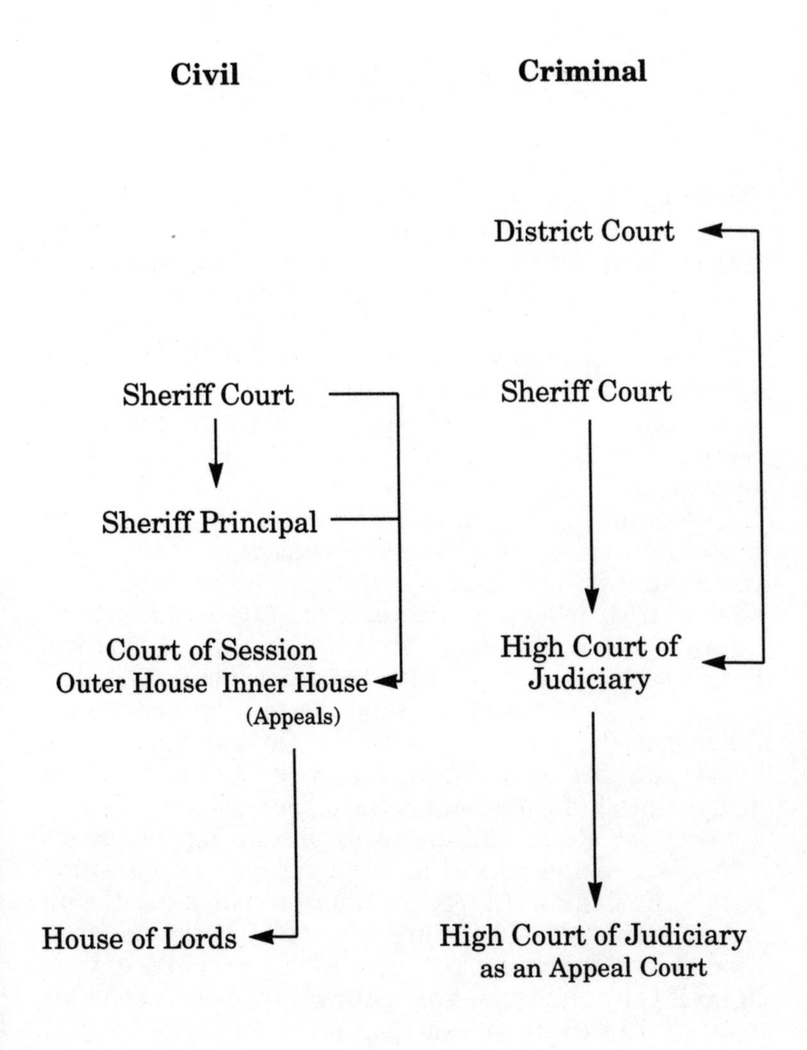

# 27 A FINAL WORD

You should bear in mind that you have no right to compensation until you have a judgment or a written agreement from the other side to pay. Your opponent's insurer may pay you compensation without a judgment, but only in order to save itself costs. It is a commercial company and has no moral obligation to you. Any expectations you might have that the insurer will have sympathy for your plight, and make an early settlement offer or interim payment, are likely to be unsatisfied.

The remedies available from the civil litigation process are rarely completely satisfactory to the parties involved. It is not at all unusual for a litigant to emerge from it feeling cheated, frustrated and angry – against his opponents, their insurers, solicitors, barrister, the judge; and even his own solicitor. Remember that the onus is on you to fully prove your claim, and that can be a tall order. Do not expect to get what you see as justice, and you will not be too disappointed. Litigation arising from a road accident is not so much about winning as about limiting your loss.

You will be surprised at what hard work pursuing your claim can be. Indeed, at times, it will seem like an ordeal. This should not put you off. Do whatever is needed to prove as much as possible for all parts of your claim if you think they are justified. Help your solicitor to bring your claim to a successful conclusion.

GOOD LUCK!

# GLOSSARY OF LEGAL TERMS

There was a time when legal language was peppered with Norman-French and medieval Latin phrases. This has mostly gone, although lawyers must still try to use language which is both precise and concise. In connection with road accidents, there are terms used by lawyers and the insurance industry, and also some general terms and abbreviations, which may require explanation, and a selection is included here.

**Advocate:** The person who represents you in court and argues your case. In Scotland, a barrister.
**Affidavit:** A sworn statement of fact or belief.
**Appellant:** The party who appeals to a higher court.
**Brief:** Concise instructions to Counsel about the case he is to present in court.
**CA:** The Court of Appeal.
**CCR:** County Court Rules, found in *The County Court Practice,* known as the green book.
**Chambers:** Judges' or barristers' rooms. Hearings of interlocutory applications and low value claims are in chambers rather than open court.
**Counsel:** A barrister.
**Counter-claim:** A claim made by the defendant against the plaintiff.
**CRU:** The Compensation Recovery Unit of the Department of Social Security (DSS).
**CSP:** Contractual sick pay, where your employer pays you sick pay under a contract which requires you to repay it from the compensation you receive.
**Curator Bonis:** In Scotland, the person through whom a person under a disability may act, a next friend.
**Damages:** Money compensation.

**Decree:** In Scotland, a judgment.

**Defendant:** The person being sued. In Scotland he is called the defender.

**Delict:** For practical purposes, the Scottish term for negligence, although, being derived from Roman law, it is not quite the same.

**Discovery:** Giving a list of the documents relating to your claim to the defendant.

**Estate:** A legal interest in property.

**Fieri facias (writ of):** (Latin – cause to be done) an order to the sheriff to execute distress on goods.

**Global offer:** All-inclusive.

**Indemnity:** Security against loss.

**Interlocutory hearing:** An application to court for directions or orders between issue of proceedings and trial.

**Interrogatories:** A list of questions to be answered on oath.

**Jurisdiction:** The authority of a court to consider any matter. The jurisdiction can be geographical, not extending beyond borders, or limited to certain types of case.

**Knock-for-knock:** An agreement between insurers to each absorb their outlay to their policyholder.

**Lawyers:** Judges, solicitors and barristers are legally qualified. Legal executives have legal training and experience, and academic lawyers are lecturers and researchers.

**Litigation:** Pursuing a claim through legal proceedings.

**Locum:** A temporary replacement doctor or solicitor (from *locum tenens* – in the place of).

**Master:** An officer of the High Court who deals with interlocutory matters.

**MIB:** The Motor Insurers' Bureau.

**Multiplicand:** An annual sum such as loss of earnings.

**Multiplier:** The number of years applying to the multiplicand.

**Personal representative:** A person who exercises the

legal rights of a person who has died, such as an executor appointed by a Will.

**Plaintiff:** The person bringing the action, the person making a complaint. In Scotland he is called the pursuer.

**Pleadings:** Brief details of the claim, and of the defence and counter-claim.

**Prejudice:** Without prejudice negotiations to not bind the parties.

**Prima facie:** (Latin – first appearance) – apparent.

**Privilege:** Documents brought into existence for the purposes of the claim are privileged in that they need not be disclosed to your opponent. This includes correspondence with your solicitor, medical reports, counsel's opinion.

**Proceedings:** A legal action.

**Quantum:** The value of a claim.

**Res ipsa loquitur:** (Latin – it speaks for itself), a phrase used in pleadings where negligence is self-evident and need not be proved.

**Respondent:** The party opposing an appeal.

**RSC:** Rules of the Supreme Court, found in *The Supreme Court Practice*, known as the white book.

**RTA:** Road traffic accident; Road Traffic Act.

**Service:** Strict rules apply to how papers are delivered to the parties to an action. They ensure that the papers come to the notice of that person in good time. There is postal service, personal service where the papers are taken to the person to be served, and substituted service on someone else such as an insurer.

**Sheriff court:** The Scottish equivalent of a county court, but which also hears criminal matters.

**Solatium:** The Scottish term for general damages.

**Split trial:** A trial on liability only, to be followed by an assessment of damages hearing if quantum cannot be agreed. Advisable where the cost of proving quantum is high but liability is in doubt.

**SSP:** Statutory sick pay, one of the state benefits recoverable by the CRU.

**Statutory:** Derived from a statue, a law passed by Parliament.
**Sue:** The act of bringing a lawsuit, a legal action.
**Taxation:** The assessment, at a special hearing, of the appropriate sum to be paid to the other party in respect of his legal costs.
**Third party:** Any person not a party to the insurance contract or covered by it; a person who is not involved in the legal action.
**ULR:** Uninsured loss recovery.

# GLOSSARY OF MEDICAL TERMS

Many medical reports are a mystery. They seem to be written for the benefit of other doctors rather than to be read and understood by the claimant, his legal advisers and the court. Here are brief definitions of some of the terms commonly found in medical reports on injuries suffered in road accidents.

**Abarticulation:** Dislocation.
**Abduction:** Moving a limb outwards.
**Ablation:** Removal.
**Acromion:** The outermost part of the shoulder.
**Acroparaesthesia:** Tingling in hands and feet.
**Adduction:** Moving a limb inwards.
**Ageusia:** Lack of sense of taste.
**Akinesia:** Loss of muscular response.
**Anemnesis:** A patient's history.
**Ankylosis:** Rigidity of a joint.
**Anosmia:** Lack of sense of smell.
**Arthritis:** Degeneration of a joint.
**Arthrodesis:** An operation to fuse a joint. This improves its stability and reduces or eliminates pain, but it is no longer a working joint.
**Arthroscopy:** Examination of a joint through a small incision.
**Articular:** Of the joint.
**Avulsion:** A tear in the layers of tissue.
**Axilla:** The armpit.
**Bilateral:** Both, for example a bilateral shoulder injury means both shoulders have a similar injury.
**Brachial plexus:** A complex network of nerves located near the armpit affecting neck, shoulder, chest and arm.

**Brachium:** Arm.
**Bursitis:** Inflammation of a bursa, a fluid pocket in tissue at some load-bearing points of the body.
**Cacosmia:** Irregularity of sense of smell.
**Callus:** Bony material which grows around the site of a fracture.
**Capsulitis:** Inflammation in and around a joint.
**Caracoid process:** Part of the shoulder blade.
**Carpus:** The bones of the wrist.
**Cartilage:** Gristle which often acts as a shock-absorber. It is not self-repairing.
**CAT scan:** Computed axial tomograph. It takes images of slices of an organ, often the brain.
**Cephalalgia:** Headache.
**Cervical:** Of the neck. There are seven cervical vertebrae, referred to in reports as C1 to C7.
**Chondromalacia:** Abnormal softness of cartilage.
**Chronic:** Slow, long-lasting.
**Cicatrix:** A scar.
**Claudication:** Lameness; limping.
**Colles' fracture:** Usually refers to a wrist fracture at the lower end of the radius bone.
**Comminuted bone:** Bone fractured into several pieces.
**Condyle:** The rounded protuberance at the end of a bone.
**Contusion:** A bruise.
**Costal:** Of the ribs.
**Coxa:** The hip.
**Cranial:** Of the brain.
**Crepitus:** Grating caused by bone rubbing on bone or hardened cartilage.
**Crural:** Of the leg.
**Cubitus:** The elbow.
**Dactylitis:** Inflammation of a finger or toe.
**Debriding:** Cleaning of a wound.
**Deltoid:** Triangular, as in the deltoid muscles of the shoulder.
**Dermatoplasty:** Skin grafting.

**Desmalgia:** Pain in a ligament.
**Diaclasia:** Surgical fracture of a bone to re-set it.
**Distal:** Extremity, the end (of a bone etc) furthest from the body.
**Dorsal spine:** Where the ribs join the spine.
**Dorsiflexion:** Backward movements of joints.
**Dorsum:** The back or outer surface, for example the back of the hand.
**ECG:** Encephalogram, a brain scan.
**EEG:** Electroencephalogram, a method of measuring brain activity.
**Effusion:** Escape of blood or other fluid into a body cavity.
**Enervation:** Weakness.
**Epiphysis:** The end of a bone, the growing part.
**Epistaxis:** A nose bleed.
**Excoriation:** Abrasion of the skin.
**Extension:** Bending backwards.
**Facet:** A small flat area on a bone, often referred to in connection with vertebrae.
**Femur:** Thigh bone.
**Fibula:** Lower leg bone, not the shin (see *Tibia*).
**Flexion:** Bending forwards.
**Fossa:** A hollow, groove or depression.
**Genicular:** Of the knee.
**Gibbus:** An angular and sharp backward curvature of the spine.
**Gonalgia:** Pain in the knee.
**Hallux:** The big toe.
**Hematoma:** A swelling containing clotted blood.
**Hemothorax:** Collection of blood in the chest cavity.
**Humerus:** Upper arm bone.
**Illium:** The large pelvic bone, the hip.
**Keloid:** Overgrowth of fibrous tissue, usually at the site of a previous injury.
**Kyphosis:** Outward curve of the spine, a hump.
**Laceration:** A ragged cut.
**Lesion:** Localized area of tissue damage.
**Ligament:** Fibrous tissue holding a joint together.

**Lordosis:** Inward curvature of the spine.
**Lumbar:** Of the lower back. The last five vertebrae of the spine, the lumbar vertebrae, are referred to in reports as L1 to L5.
**Mala:** Cheekbone.
**Malleolus:** The ankle fulcrum bone.
**Maxilla:** Either of the two bones of the upper jaw.
**McMurray's test:** A test to detect tearing of the knee cartilage.
**Meniscus:** Crescent-shaped, often referring to cartilage in the knee joint.
**Metacarpals:** Hand bones.
**Metatarsals:** Foot bones.
**MRI scan:** Magnetic Resonance imaging, considered better than X-rays.
**Myodynia:** Muscle pain.
**Neuropraxia:** Tingling, weakness and numbness due to loss of nerve function.
**NMR scan:** Nuclear magnetic resonance (another term for MRI).
**Occiput:** Back of the head.
**Oedema:** Swelling.
**Orbit:** Eye socket.
**Osteoarthritis:** Degenerative disease of the joint affecting the cartilage.
**Osteoarthrotomy:** An operation to remove bone around a joint.
**Osteochondritis:** Inflammation of a bone.
**Palmarflexion:** Bending the wrist towards arm.
**Paraethesia:** The sensation known as pins and needles.
**Paraplegia:** Paralysis of lower part of the body.
**Patella:** Kneecap.
**Phalanges:** Finger bones.
**Plantar:** The sole of the foot.
**Pneumothorax:** Air in the chest cavity.
**Prognosis:** The expected course of the injury and the prospects for recovery.
**Prolapse:** slipping down or displacement as with an

intervertebral disc.
**Prone:** Lying face down.
**Proximate:** Near. Opposite of distal.
**Quadriplegia:** Paralysis of arms and legs.
**Rachialgia:** Spinal pain.
**Radius:** Outer or front forearm bone.
**Reduction:** Bringing back to normal position.
**Rima:** A crack.
**Sacrum:** The five fused vertebrae which join the spine to the pelvic girdle.
**Sartorius:** Thigh muscle.
**Scapula:** Shoulder blade.
**Sciatica:** Pain in the sciatic nerve down the back of the leg.
**Scoliosis:** A twisted vertebra.
**Septum:** A partition of tissue separating cavities, as in nasal septum.
**Spondyl:** A vertebra.
**Spondylosis:** Arthritis of the spine.
**Sternum:** Breastbone.
**Subluxation:** Partial dislocation of a joint.
**Supine:** Lying face upwards.
**Synovitis:** Inflammation of a joint lining.
**Tallus:** The ankle.
**Tendon:** Fibrous tissue which anchors muscles.
**Tendonitis:** Inflammation of a tendon.
**Tenoplasty:** Operation to repair a tendon.
**Tenosynovitis:** Inflammation of a tendon's sheath.
**Tetraplegia:** Another term for quadriplegia.
**Thoracic:** Of the chest or mid trunk. There are twelve thoracic vertebrae, referred to in reports as T1 to T12.
**Tibia:** Shin bone.
**Tinnitus:** Noises in the ear.
**Trapezius:** A large kite-shaped muscle reaching from the back of the head down the back and out to the shoulders.
**Tuberosity:** The rounded end of bones.
**Ulna:** Inner or rear forearm bone.
**Vascular:** Of blood vessels and circulation.

**Vertebrae:** The bones of the spine.
**Whiplash:** A hyperextension injury usually affecting muscles and soft tissue around the spine and shoulders. It is caused by a violent reversal of movement of the body, a whipping movement.
**Zygoma:** Part of the cheek bone.

# CLAIM QUESTIONNAIRE

If you are involved in an accident, you will be asked for a great many details about yourself, the accident, your losses and any early medical treatment. You may be asked for your insurance details at the scene of the accident by the other driver or the police. Your solicitor will ask you to complete a detailed questionnaire which will be the initial instructions to him to begin investigating your claim. All this comes at a time when you may be very distressed and confused, and you may have difficulty remembering the details which are asked for, or even where to find them.

Here is a sample questionnaire which you can complete at your leisure with relevant details known to you now. If you do this in pencil, you can amend them when they change. If you keep this book in your car, you then have some essential details to hand if you are involved in an accident, and you can enter details of the other driver, witnesses, police officer attending and accident circumstances while it is all fresh. It will act as a prompt sheet, and important details will not be lost because of a failure of memory.

## *Personal details*

Full Name: ..............................................................................
Address: ..................................................................................
...................................................................................................
Telephone No. (Home): ..........................................................
Telephone No. (Work): ..........................................................
Date of Birth: .........................................................................
This is required to establish legal capacity and must be included in pleadings. It may also have an effect on a claim

for lost earnings (approaching retirement).

Occupation: ........................................................................
Name and Address of employer: ..................................
.........................................................................................
.........................................................................................
Clock/works No.: .............................................................
These details are required in order to obtain evidence of loss of earnings.

VAT No. (if registered): ..................................................
The recoverable cost of vehicle repairs may be net of VAT as you can claim it back if vehicle used for business.

National Insurance No.: ...................................................
This will be needed to register your claim with the CRU.

Your Vehicle: Make: ..........................................................
Model: ............................ Reg. No.: ...............................
Colour:..............................................................................
Witnesses often identify cars by their colour rather than by make or registration number.

Insurance company:
Policy No.: .......................................................................
Type of Policy: Comprehensive
Third Party Fire and Theft
Third Party Only
Name of Policyholder: .......................................................
This is the name known to your insurance company.

***Accident details***

Date: ..................................... Time: ..............................
Location: ...........................................................................
.........................................................................................
Be precise, give the street/road name, town, location in street in relation to a feature e.g. High Street, Preston, Lancs, just past the Kings Head pub on the Bridge Street side.

Weather conditions: ..........................................................................
..........................................................................................
..........................................................................................
Lighting: .................................................................................
Road conditions: .....................................................................
..........................................................................................
Brief description of accident circumstances: ..................
..........................................................................................
..........................................................................................
..........................................................................................
..........................................................................................
..........................................................................................
Sketch plan of accident site showing paths taken by all vehicles involved:

Other Driver: his/her vehicle:
Make: .................................. Model: ................................
Reg. No.: ............................ Colour: ..............................
Other driver's name: ..........................................................
Address: .................................................................................
..........................................................................................
Description: ...........................................................................
..........................................................................................
Approximate age, race, hair, obvious occupation e.g. postman. Drivers often later claim that they were not the person who was driving the car at the time of the accident.

If driving employer's vehicle:
Employer's name: ...........................................................................
Address: ....................................................................................
......................................................................................................
Vehicle's owner if not driver or employer:
Name: ........................................................................................
Address: ....................................................................................
......................................................................................................
Insurance company: ......................................................................
Policy No.: .................................................................................

Independent witnesses:
1 Name: ...................................................................................
Address: ..............................................................................
..............................................................................................
Description: .........................................................................

2 Name: ...................................................................................
Address: ..............................................................................
..............................................................................................
Description: .........................................................................

3 Name: ...................................................................................
Address: ..............................................................................
..............................................................................................
Description: .........................................................................

If police attended:
Name, number and station of officer(s) attending:
......................................................................................................
......................................................................................................
If accident reported to police other than at accident scene:
Name and address of police station where reported:
......................................................................................................
Name and number of officer who took details:
......................................................................................................
Words of admission spoken by other driver:
......................................................................................................

***Vehicle damage***

Location and extent of damage:
e.g. heavy – front nearside wing: light – rear offside door ..................................................................................
Vehicle recovered from scene by : ....................................
......................................................................................
Vehicle stored by : ..............................................................
......................................................................................
From : ................................ to : ......................................
Date of settlement of repair or vehicle value by own insurer (comprehensive policies) .....................................

***Details of injuries***

Driver:
Name: ..................................................................................
Address: ..............................................................................
......................................................................................
......................................................................................
Date of birth: ......................................................................
Nature of injuries: ..............................................................
......................................................................................
......................................................................................
Name and Address of GP: ..................................................
......................................................................................
......................................................................................
If attended hospital:
Name and address of hospital:..........................................
......................................................................................
......................................................................................
Date attended: ....................................................................
Treatment received: ..........................................................
......................................................................................
X-rays taken of: ..................................................................

***Passengers***

1 Name : ..............................................................................
Address: ..............................................................................
......................................................................................
Age: ..................................... (if child or elderly adult)

Where seated in vehicle: ..............................................

2 Name: ..................................................................
Address: ..............................................................
..........................................................................
Age: ..........Where seated in vehicle: ............................

3 Name: ..................................................................
Address: ..............................................................
..........................................................................
Age: ..........Where seated in vehicle: ............................

## Other losses

***Other property damage***

| Item | when obtained | type of damage | replacement cost |
|---|---|---|---|

***Travel expenses***

Car hire:
from..................... to....................... cost.......................
Hire company name: ..............................................
from..................... to....................... cost.......................
Hire company name: ..............................................

Other travel:
Give dates and purpose of journey if possible
Bus

Rail

Taxi

***Medical expenses***
Prescriptions:

| Item | Date | Cost |
|---|---|---|

Physiotherapy or other treatment:

| Date | Treatment | Practitioner | Cost |
|---|---|---|---|

***Loss of earnings***

| Nature of loss<br>e.g. overtime/bonus | Dates from – to | Amount |
|---|---|---|

# USEFUL ADDRESSES

**The Law Society**, 110–113 Chancery Lane, London WC2A 1PL

**The Law Society of Scotland**, 26 Drumsheugh Gardens, Edinburgh EH3 7YR

**The Law Society of Northern Ireland**, 90 Victoria Street, Belfast BT1 3JZ

**The General Council of the Bar**, 3 Bedford Row, London WC1R 4DB

**The Institute of Legal Executives**, Kempston Manor, Kempston, Beds MK42 7AB

**The Motor Insurers' Bureau**, 152 Silbury Boulevard, Central Milton Keynes MK9 1NB

**Legal Aid Board Head Office**, 85 Gray's Inn Road, London WC1X 8AA

**The Policyholders' Protection Board**, 51 Gresham Street, London EC2V 7HQ

**The Solicitors Complaints Bureau**, Victoria Court, 8 Dormer Place, Leamington Spa, Warwick CV32 5AE

**Lord Chancellor's Department**, Trevelyn House, Great Peter Street, London SW1P 2BY

**Court of Protection**, Protection Division, Public Trust Office, Stewart House, Kingsway, London WC2B 6JX

**The Accident Line**, Freephone: 050 019 2939

**The Insurance Ombudsman Bureau**, 135 Park Street, London SE1 9AE

**The Office of the Legal Services Ombudsman**, 22 Oxford Court, Oxford Street, Manchester M2 3WQ

**The Compensation Recovery Unit** For England, Wales and Scotland: Department of Social Security, Compensation Recovery Unit, Reyrolle Building, Hebburn, Tyne & Wear NE31 1XB

For Northern Ireland: Department of Health and Social Services, Compensation Recovery Unit, Castle Buildings, Stormont, Belfast BT4 3RA

# BIBLIOGRAPHY

This book has been written to meet the need for a concise guide to claiming compensation after a road accident. I have tried to make the legal and procedural complexities of dealing with the consequences of the accident easy to understand. All other books on the subject which I know of have been written specifically for lawyers, but you may find some of the following titles useful to refer to. Your public library should have some of them in the reference section, or it may be able to get them for you. If you know anyone who is at university, they may have access to a law library.

Bingham & Berrymans' *Motor Claims Cases*, 10th edn (Butterworths, 1994). A very useful book containing details of road accident cases which indicate how the courts decide who was negligent.

Goldrein & de Haas (eds), *Butterworths Personal Injury Litigation Service* A three-volume loose-leaf work with regular updating supplements. It covers liability and quantum, citing cases in support.

The Judicial Studies Board, *General Damages in Personal Injury Cases,* 2nd edn (Blackstone Press, 1994). This gives the broad brackets of the value of compensation into which most personal injury claims will fall. It is the starting-point for lawyers and the courts when assessing damages for injury.

*Legal Aid Handbook* (Sweet & Maxwell). Published annually.

Pritchard, John, and Solomon, Nicola, *Personal Injury Litigation*, 8th edn (FT Law & Tax,1995). This deals with the law, evidence and procedure in all personal injury claims including accidents at work.

Kemp & Kemp, *The Quantum of Damages* (Sweet & Maxwell). This has brief details of cases giving the award of damages, or supporting or against particular items of claim. Three volumes in loose-leaf format with regular updating supplements.

Thompson (general ed.), *The County Court Practice* (Butterworths). The 'green book', published annually and containing the county court rules with commentary.

Jacob (general ed.), *The Supreme Court Practice* (Sweet & Maxwell). The 'white book' containing the rules of the Supreme Court with commentary. This is for High Court and appeal matters but also applies in the county court where there is no equivalent county court rule.

*Current Law* (Sweet & Maxwell). A monthly journal of new legislation and notable cases.

Duncan, M., & Marsh, C., *Fatal Accident Claims* (Fourmat Publishing, 1993)

Goldrein & de Haas, *Structured Settlements – A Practical Guide* (Butterworths, 1993)

*Charlesworth & Percy on Negligence*, 8th edn (Sweet & Maxwell, 1990)

# INDEX